Today is the era of the aggressive but often misinformed atheist. Misunderstandings and half-truths abound about how we got the Bible, how well preserved it is, whether or not it is full of contradictions, whether the resurrection is credible, and more. Köstenberger, Bock, and Chatraw set the record straight in a way that ordinary people can readily understand. Must reading for anyone with questions about these and related subjects or who knows anyone with questions about them!

—Craig L. Blomberg, Distinguished Professor of New
Testament, Denver Seminary

We will soon be packing her bags, loading the car, and driving our eighteen-year-old daughter to a major state university known for its liberalism, in a city known for "keeping it weird," at a time when truth is being redefined! I was going to ask Andreas Köstenberger, Darrell Bock, and Josh Chatraw if I could send them with her, but now that they have written this book, I will send it instead. These three are a rarity: top notch scholars with a heart for real people and a style that is eminently accessible. This latest work came just in time for me, and for you, and your kids too!

—Pete Briscoe, senior pastor, Bent Tree Fellowship,
Carrolton, Texas

Truth Matters should be on every college freshman's reading list. The authors square off with today's leading skeptics of Christianity, offering convincing counter arguments in an easy-to-read style. Although written for college students, the book's rich content makes it an excellent resource for adults of all ages as they encounter questions about the trustworthiness of the Bible and the truthfulness of Christianity.

—Lynn H. Cohick, professor of New Testament,
Wheaton College

For too long our churches have crossed their fingers and sent their youth off to Lion's Den University offering little more than encouragements to hold on to a "blind faith" and to simply ignore the arguments of non-Christian professors. "What do they know?" I remember hearing. Well, the honest answer is, "A lot!" This book is a welcome help for students who would rather have a reasoned faith than a blind one—a faith that seeks to face with confidence, rather than ignore in fear, the hard questions posed by professors, peers, or even their own doubts. With honesty, humility, and winsomeness, the authors help us to see the overlooked complexities behind the often simplistic arguments against our faith, giving us permission to pull our fingers from our ears AND still have faith in Christ. An excellent resource for my students (and their parents, pastors, and younger siblings too)!

—Eric Gambardella, campus staff, InterVarsity Christian Fellowship, Christopher Newport University

What I love about this book is that it is both intellectually responsible and imminently readable. I anticipate it becoming one of my most recommended resources, both for students struggling with challenges to their faith as well as seekers asking honest questions.

—J. D. Greear, author of *Stop Asking Jesus Into Your Heart* and *Gospel: Recovering the Power that Made Christianity Revolutionary*

This is a very timely book. Over the last few years, a number of critical scholars, including Bart Ehrman, have attacked the historicity and reliability of the New Testament and have made claims that simply cannot be supported by the evidence. This book sets the records straight. In a fashion that is both scholarly and accessible, the authors have provided a tremendous resource for the church.

—Michael J. Kruger, president and professor of New Testament, Reformed Theological Seminary

I have worked with university students for over twenty years, serving in three different states, and the level of skepticism has never been higher. This is due, in part, to the aggressive secular agenda that is promoted from the first day of orientation until the final graduation speech is delivered. This book will without question serve as a valuable resource and is a must read for our staff and students in Raleigh-Durham and around the world.

—Rupert Leary, Campus Outreach Global Ministries

There has been a need for this book to be written for a long time. I'm thrilled to see it finally in print! *Truth Matters* offers cogent responses to some of the most common objections against Christianity. I will be recommending this book to students for a long time.

—Sean McDowell, apologetics expert and coauthor of
Is God Just A Human Invention?

After fifteen years ministering to the millennial generation and their families, one thing has remained constant: the need to logically and practically prepare students to respond to views opposing Christianity and the Bible. Köstenberger, Bock, and Chatraw have provided an accessible and practical guide of strong arguments for the Christian faith and successfully counter popular arguments against orthodox Christianity. Get this book for your teenager, your college student, or your minister to students. Their faith may depend on it.

—Dave Miller, lead pastor, Sentral Church,
Oklahoma City, Oklahoma

Truth Matters is a wonderfully accessible, yet in-depth reply to some of the most common criticisms of Christianity that contemporary culture launches our way. The authors are fair and even-handed in the way they portray Bart Ehrmann, yet offer insightful critique of both his views and the spirit of skepticism that he represents. This is a very useful work for followers of Jesus at any age, but particularly high school and college students. I look forward to the more detailed volume that follows up on this one.

—Scott B. Rae, Dean of Faculty, Chair of Philosophy
Department, Talbot School of Theology, Biola University

Steeped in the soup of postmodernism's insidious skepticism, our youth and young adults are floundering in their commitments to God. Recent renewed attacks on the veracity and reliability of the Bible and its message have shipwrecked the faith of many Christians who are ill-equipped to stand their ground and defend their beliefs. *Truth Matters* delivers a scholarly response to these challenges and provides the believer with reasoned arguments to effectively counter the onslaught they are facing today. In a very readable format, Köstenberger, Bock, and Chatraw have provided the information necessary "to make a defense to everyone who asks you to give an account for the hope that is in you."

—Jay Sedwick, professor of Educational Ministries and
Leadership, Dallas Theological Seminary

Truth Matters is a godsend, a clear and accessible resource for equipping Christian students to survive—and thrive—in our increasingly skeptical culture. The tone of this book is light and playful enough to engage the average high school student, but its evidence and arguments are sturdy enough to provide solid ground for anyone seeking to respond intelligently to modern attacks on the Christian faith. With a clear mastery of the evidence and a keen insight into how to address the "hot topics" of modern skepticism, *Truth Matters* will both encourage and equip. This is a must-have resource for Christian students, youth pastors, and parents.

—Craig A. Smith, youth speaker and adjunct professor of
New Testament and Christian Doctrine,
Denver Seminary

Truth Matters is a timely resource that students need to have in their hands. Throughout this book students will be challenged to think through key components of their faith while being equipped to defend that faith in their culture. Most important, I believe that as students engage with this material their faith will be strengthened and they will fall more in love with their Savior.

—Ben Trueblood, director of LifeWay Student Ministry

Truth-telling about the Bible matters, especially in an increasingly post-modern and cynical culture, binging on spin-doctoring about all subjects imaginable. Köstenberger, Bock, and Chatraw have done us all a great service in providing some straightforward answers to the usual hard questions people ask about the Bible. Especially helpful in a biblically illiterate culture is their treatment of the usual things trotted out by pundits who seek to demonstrate that the Bible is riddled with errors, inconsistencies, and just plain myths. As it turns out, that is not the truth about the Truth.

—Ben Witherington, III, Amos Professor for Doctoral
Studies, Asbury Theological Seminary

This book plays hardball with the flippant scholarly pretensions of certain professors and publications. Yet it makes its case for the truth of the gospel and the Bible in measured, charitable, and nurturing ways. Without claiming too much for facts and argument, the authors encourage an informed Christian faith that is reasoned, not blind. Nor do they lose sight of the living dynamic of God—Father, Son, and Spirit—and holy Scripture in sustaining saving faith. Readable, reliable, and responsible, this book deserves a wide readership, particularly among those wishing to learn loyalty to Christ in the face of scholarly manipulation of historic witness about him.

—Robert W. Yarbrough, professor of New Testament,
Covenant Theological Seminary

TRUTH

Matters

CONFIDENT
FAITH *in a*
CONFUSING
WORLD

Andreas Köstenberger,
Darrell Bock, & Josh Chatraw

PUBLISHING GROUP

NASHVILLE, TENNESSEE

978-1-4336-8226-1

Published by B&H Publishing Group
Nashville, Tennessee

Dewey Decimal Classification: 230
Subject Heading: FAITH \ TRUTH \ APOLOGETICS

4 5 6 7 8 9 10 • 19 18 17 16 15

Dedication

From Andreas:

For my daughter Lauren at the occasion of your graduation from UNC-Chapel Hill. Well done!

And for Tahlia as you start your college journey at NC State. Keep loving Jesus and loving people.

I love you girls!

From Darrell:

To my students at DTS, Talbot, and Western, who ask questions about how the Bible really works and are patient about the answers to such questions.

From Josh:

For my children Addison and Hudson because one day you will need this book.

Contents

"It's a dangerous business, Frodo, going out your door. You step onto the road, and if you don't keep your feet, there's no knowing where you might be swept off to."
—J. R. R. TOLKIEN, *THE LORD OF THE RINGS*

Skepticism 101

We're not in Sunday school anymore, Dorothy.

This is 9:15, Monday-Wednesday-Friday, sandwiched between a short night's sleep and your 10:30 college algebra, with little more than a gobbled-down granola bar to help prepare you for what's coming next this morning.

David and Goliath can't help you here. If you expect to keep your head above water in this class, you'll need a lot more than Noah's ark—and certainly more than the catchy lyrics from a three-chord worship song you learned at church last week. You're about to face a religion professor who's actually better at arguing your case for the validity of Christian faith than you are. And when his spiritually shocking lectures start turning into assignments for thousand-word papers and midterm exams, he won't be taking your favorite Bible verse for an answer.

What will you do then?

More disturbingly, who will you *be* then . . . when all this is over?

Because even if you sit in the back, trying hard not to believe what's coming out of his mouth, that doesn't mean you won't be led to wonder if what you always thought to be true was just a narrow, sentimental way of looking at things. Just because you feel strong in your faith today doesn't mean you can't be convinced he's making good sense, given the right conditions and the wrong conclusions. Exposed to enough doubts, anyone can be swayed in the subtle direction of disbelief, choosing to live out what your instructor would call a more sensible, less gullible life.

Students, meet Dr. Bart Ehrman, one of the leading voices attacking the reliability of the Christian faith, and many others like him who teach about early Christianity in various locales around the country. And prepare to say good-bye to what you always thought about God and the Bible.

———————

Whether or not you've spent much time in your life wrestling with religious questions, it's time you started thinking beyond the five loaves and two fish of biblical faith—not just because you need to know but because your life may one day depend on realizing how solid the ground beneath your Christian beliefs actually is. What do you do when the Bible goes from being the answer to being the question? How can you discuss its contents when its contents are being questioned as made up or having nothing to do with what really happened? How can you begin to develop a confident faith in such a confusing world?

Oh, and one other reason: because the Bart Ehrmans of this world are waiting for you. Whether you attend college or not, his philosophy is popular in our culture, and it will undermine your faith as a Christian if you are not prepared.

Ehrman is really one sharp guy. No doubt about that. You may have seen him on prime-time television, breezily bantering with the likes of Jon Stewart and Stephen Colbert. You may have read or heard about his growing number of *New York Times* best-selling books, covering the subjects of biblical authenticity and the existence of Jesus. You may have seen one or more of his debate performances against scholars who oppose his agnostic views. Or honestly, perhaps you've never heard of him at all.

But that's OK because this book is not about Bart Ehrman. This book is about God and his truth in a changing world and shifting culture. It is about you and your experience with your own personal assortment of skeptical voices and authority figures. And there's a good chance you will face the same questions and arguments that have thrust Ehrman into the cultural jet stream of Christian doubt. That's why we've decided to arrange this book loosely around the issues he is popularizing and perpetuating through his teaching and writing.

He claims, for example, that the gospel is not really based on what Jesus said or taught to his disciples but gradually evolved and emerged as simply the loudest, majority voice during the first few centuries of the Christian era. By seizing the political and religious high ground and declaring its writings as holy Scripture, Christianity shut down the healthy voices of diversity and strong-armed them into silence.

The Bible was put together to suit an agenda.

He maintains that many of the claims of the New Testament were fabricated and not actually written by the traditional authors to which they are ascribed.

The Bible is basically a forgery.

He claims that the copying process which preserved the writings of Scripture throughout the early centuries AD has left the surviving manuscripts with so many errors and discrepancies—some accidental, some intentional—that we can place no degree of confidence in our ability to determine what the original documents actually said.

Your Bible doesn't contain the real words of God after all.

He claims Scripture is so shot through with contradictions, competing theologies, and unclear time lines of what happened when, we'd be crazy to think we can trust it to give us authoritative, accurate information about its core claims.

The Bible can't seem to keep its own story straight.

He states that Christ's disciples believed something miraculous happened to the crucified Jesus, but we really cannot know for certain that what they claim is historical fact.

The whole basis of Christianity is in question.

More important than everything else, he claims the so-called God behind this whole charade is hardly worthy of his compassionate or all-powerful reputation, not when we sweep an objective radar across the world, picking up more signals of pain and suffering in the human experience than we can even begin to explain or process.

God doesn't care. Maybe God isn't even there.

It's all a scheme. All a sham. All smoke and mirrors. No truth, just misplaced, ultimately empty hopefulness.

Try waking up to the smell of that coffee three mornings a week across campus, and being someone who learned most of what you know about Jesus from a character in a Mel Gibson movie, or by being pretty sure you feel God in your heart when you pray a certain way or listen to Christian music while you're running.

Nothing wrong, obviously, in coloring your life with popular, faith-based influences like these. But this low level of biblical knowledge simply won't cut it in your college religion classes. And not when the questions of life grow too complex to be answered anymore with crayons and church scissors, or with campouts and weekend retreats.

If you still want to be standing upright when the pillars of your faith are rocked repeatedly back and forth, when everything you've believed about God and the Bible is called into mocking question—two or three periods a week, for a full hour at a time—then you desperately need the information you're about to read. You don't need to cower like Ehrman's description of other baby-faced students in his classes who "cover their ears and hum loudly so that they don't have to hear anything that might cause them to doubt their cherished belief."[1]

Trust us, your "cherished belief" can stack up to his doubts. With your eyes and your ears wide open.

So this is not a personal attack, but it is a personal cause. And if you'll read on, we believe you'll enjoy being able to counter some of these bold, disbelieving assertions with your own brand of boldness and confidence. You'll discover the kind of biblical background, answers, and thinking skills that can give you a calm, reasoned strength in the midst of skeptical sarcasm and attack.

These things matter. The truth stands up. And you're smart to be here in this book right now rather than wherever else you could be . . . because knowing what you believe and why you believe it can add an element of real courage to your heart of Christian faith and love.

> *The first to state his case seems right until*
> *another comes and cross-examines him.*
> PROVERBS 18:17

The Skeptical Mystique

What Makes Unbelief So Terribly Believable?

I suppose at the end of the day I simply trust human intelligence. Anyone should be able to see whether a point of view is plausible or absurd, whether a historical claim has merit or is pure fantasy driven by an ideological or theological desire for a certain set of answers to be right.
—BART EHRMAN[1]

[Love] rejoices in the truth.
—PAUL THE APOSTLE (1 COR. 13:6)

By the time Bart Ehrman emerged from Princeton Seminary with his master of divinity and Ph.D. degrees, he was no longer the fundamentalist Christian he believed himself to be when he entered Moody Bible Institute as an undergrad. Nor was he the revised evangelical version he had become while completing his bachelor's work at Wheaton College, another respected Christian school in the Chicago area.

Instead, during his years of postgraduate study, he did what he claims few other conservative Christians are willing to do: plow head first into the biblical evidence, letting it take him wherever it leads rather than forcing it to conform to his own preconceived biases and assumptions. He maintains that if the rest of us were prepared to do this, we would come to the same, inescapable conclusions he did. We would realize from a combination of hard proof and missing links that the Bible cannot really be trusted, no matter how badly we may wish it to be true. And we would see all our nice little well-meaning Christian beliefs for the childish notions they really are.

Ehrman lost his faith after engaging in enough of these scholarly skirmishes. And he's been filching it from unsuspecting students ever since.

What is it, though, that makes his voice so credible? What turns a full-time religion professor (University of North Carolina, with an adjunct professorship at Duke University) into an academic rock star? How has he succeeded at moving hundreds of thousands of books—four titles on the *New York Times* list in the last nine years[2]—when most other treatises on biblical history and hypothesis succeed at little more than curing their readers' insomnia?

What is he selling that so many people are buying?

And what can you learn from the answers to these questions, in hopes that you won't be drawn into the same fog of doubt and skepticism?

Here are four general, introductory observations, as well as some practical heads-up and takeaways, to help you see why skeptical professors succeed at making short work of so many students—and why you don't need to be one of them. Not all of these tactics are wrong or underhanded in themselves, but you still need to be aware of them because they can easily be turned into points of entry to shape the way you receive information, giving doubt a softer, more agreeable place to land.

When You Put It That Way . . .

First, *they speak your language.* Ehrman, for example, comes at you with a story—very compelling—of how he gravitated toward Christian belief as a needy teenager, not far distant from the age and life experience of his college students. But his youthful, emotional zeal could only hold him for so long. What the church had done temporarily to satisfy his adolescent insecurities, he eventually found satisfied by academia and intellectual pursuits, until suddenly—finally—life began to make a lot more sense. Doubts that he had shushed away during his more faith-infused moments would no longer stay quiet. *Of course* the Bible is a man-made document, he reasoned. *Of course* God can't be who the Bible claims him to be. *Of course* a man can't come back from the dead. *Of course* there shouldn't be such a vast difference between the version of reality the Bible paints and the one that swirls around us every day down here where we can see it and live it and smell it.

He's not the only one, obviously, who experienced an agnostic epiphany during one of these wrestling matches, what he might call a head-clearing breath of intellectual honesty. But unlike the crusty, hardened image of the stereotypical skeptic, Ehrman doesn't come off as cold, angry, and argumentative. In fact, he's not above being surprisingly charming and vulnerable, admitting that he occasionally wakes up in a cold sweat in the middle of the night, panicked at the prospect that perhaps he is wrong, perhaps hell is real, and perhaps he and others who've jettisoned their Christian faith midstream are in for some big trouble down the line.[3]

He went on to do some personal grappling in his life with the issue of suffering and tragedy, struggling as many of us do to understand where God is when we're hurting, when it seems he could do something about it if he wanted to. Who among us hasn't tried to square how a good God can seem to so quietly, callously stand by while his creation is falling apart—while forty people plunge to their deaths in a freak bridge collapse in China, while a young single woman is raped along a wooded jogging trail in Pennsylvania, while children are shot in their classrooms in Connecticut by a gun-wielding lunatic, or tornadoes in Oklahoma devastate two elementary schools?

Good questions. Worth asking.

Most of us expect philosophical and doctrinal debates to occur within the stuffy air of intangible theories or amid the noisy clash of talking heads, picket signs, and television cameras. But wrap these same kinds of proceedings in the warm cloth and colors of a moving, personal story line, and the whole mood of the room changes. Guards and defenses come down. Now people are listening. Sympathizing. Laughing. Perhaps even nodding along, despite their confused, questioning disagreement inside.

They at least see where this person is coming from. Today we meet more people who have a story about how God let them down. Their faith was shaken to the core, and they are left with pain and doubt.

Again, not that there's anything wrong with stepping out from behind the curtain of ideas to let your audience look into your eyes, hear your story, and see you as a real person. But an appealing narrative does not negate the role of *truth* as being the ultimate arbiter between competing lines of thought. Whether the engaging speaker is an agnostic New Testament professor or a tattooed guest pastor speaking every night of the week at church youth camp, the same standards of listening for truth still apply, no matter how much you may like the guy personally or feel he gets you.

It's not how they say it; it's what they're saying.

I Didn't Know That

Second, *they know you've probably never contemplated these ideas before.* The average person, even the average college student who's spent their whole life in church, hasn't invested a lot of time dwelling on the Bible's origins or scouring the history pages of Christianity. They know only (or at least mainly) what their personal experiences with God have been like, but these alone are enough to leave them feeling fairly well versed in what's most important about Christian faith. More than economics class or speech class, they come into *this* class with a range of deep, familiar understandings and memories about God that lead them to believe they've probably covered most of this material already when they were kids in vacation Bible school.

What a shock when the popsicles their new professor serves up don't taste like those at all.

So for many this person becomes (like Ehrman) the witty tour guide, showing them around some fields of subject matter loaded with new sights and sounds and far more fascinating on the inside than they typically appear from the outside. You'll get no argument from us on that.

The problem is that the tour guide—who correctly presumes his tour group probably doesn't have the foggiest idea what they're looking at—is in the enviable position of being able to choose the places you visit and what he wants to highlight about each one. As a result his rhetoric and interpretations of religious material all too often *conceal* a lot more than they *reveal*. And few if any in the classroom know enough to know the difference.

One of the things you really notice in Ehrman's writings, for example—if you're looking carefully—is that he rarely acknowledges counterarguments to his own positions. His treatments of issues are usually far more one-sided than the real discussion that's taking place out here in the broader arena of religious scholarship.

He might take you, for example, into an interesting exhibit on biblical manuscripts and artifacts, unveiling a world of scribes and ancient parchments. But he'll only show you enough evidence to help back up his claim that our modern-day Bibles can't possibly be based on the original words of Scripture—if this is the shoddy method for how God handed down his holy words to us.[4] He apparently assumes that simply by raising questions he's giving you the only answers you should be willing to accept. Not so. Saying that the Bible *could* contain errors is a long way from proving it *does*. Just because a person says something *might* be true doesn't necessarily mean it *is*.

But that's how it's done in many college classrooms, where seats on the Skeptical Biblical Tour bus head out every hour on the hour. They know it's probably your first time going. They know they can fill up the whole class period pointing out all kinds of reasons for you *not* to trust the Bible. They also know the tour booklet you're carrying (the textbook they've chosen) will back them up on everything they're saying and showing you. And if you don't have any real foundation in disputing or dealing with the various biblical or theological topics they're raising, you're likely to think, well . . . , *This guy sure sounds pretty convincing to me.*

But they know better. They know that whether writing a book or presenting a paper or lecturing in a college class, any work of scholarship should set out to defend its position against the best of all opposing positions. Instead of hoping nobody looks over and says, "Hey, if what you're saying is true, then what do you make of *that*—over *there*?" A fair-minded tour guide will want to take you around to all the exhibits, making sure you hear what everybody else is saying (even their critics), convinced that his or her arguments are stout enough to lick those of any challenger.

If you're only hearing one side of the story or a narrow selection of sides—especially when the presenter knows you're perhaps completely new to the line of study he's bringing up—then you need to wonder *why* he's not telling you *what* he's not telling you, and how come he's so careful not to show you the rest.

My Thoughts Exactly

Third, *they comfort and confirm an air of disbelief.* You probably don't need any convincing that we live in an age when about the only belief you'll be frowned upon for having is one that doesn't allow for complete diversity, in which everyone's chosen ways lead ultimately to truth. *Their* truth.

A recent Harvard graduate, quoted in D. A. Carson's book *The Intolerance of Tolerance,* made this point in a speech delivered at commencement: "They tell us it's heresy to suggest the superiority of some value, fantasy to believe in moral argument, slavery to submit to a judgment sounder than our own. The freedom of our day is *freedom to devote ourselves to any values we please, on the mere condition that we do not believe them to be true.*"[5]

You might want to read that again. It's quite profound.

Most people today have bought into the tolerance mind-set entirely. They feel inherently resistant to the exclusive truth claims of Christianity—such as belief in Jesus as being the only means of salvation—and they'll lap up what anybody says that reinforces their own personal decision to depart from their religious upbringing or to procure an open-minded reputation.

Tolerance has become such a god in our culture that not to have it is heresy. The effect is that tolerance swallows up truth, negating any need to search for things that might offend or challenge our preferences. It conveniently avoids the notion that certain things might just apply to all of us, no matter who we are or what we believe. It is a comfortable place to be, for it challenges nothing but truth, but it may also be a dangerous home to inhabit.

So when someone injects his or her brand of skeptical sarcasm into the discussion, they are speaking to a friendly court. They sound reasonable, especially now that you're out on your own, out from under your parents' eye and expectations. They know that you probably don't need to take too many more steps down the ladder of doubt before they convince you not only that Christianity is merely one choice among many but that it's not really a viable option of belief at all. As Ehrman himself ultimately concluded: "I don't 'know' if there is a God; but I think that if there is one, he certainly isn't the one proclaimed by the Judeo-Christian tradition."[6]

Your friends or a professor share these same sentiments.

And if so, they will want you to know that it is OK to doubt your faith. They will question why you are still trying to hang on to your shaken Christian beliefs, and you may find that they will throw the alleged weight of the entire academic community behind their arguments, as Ehrman does in the opening chapter of *Jesus, Interrupted:* "All of my closest friends (and next-to-closest friends) in the guild of New Testament studies agree with most of my historical views of the New Testament, the historical Jesus, the development of the Christian faith, and other similar issues. We may disagree on this point or that (in fact we do—we are, after all, scholars), but we all agree on the historical methods and the basic conclusions they lead to."[7]

Everybody else agrees with me.

Everybody? Really?

They'd like you to believe that among people who really know what they're talking about, the skeptical viewpoint toward the reliability of the Bible, the claims of Jesus, and the existence of God is standard fare. They want you to think that what they're presenting as enlightened conclusions are the accepted baseline, the boiler plate. "We all agree." *All of us.*

But no matter what anybody says, we promise you that those who hold such views are not the only people doing serious work in biblical studies.

> Of all the ATS-accredited seminaries in the United States, the top ten largest seminaries are all evangelical. These seminaries represent thousands and thousands of students, and hundreds and hundreds of professors. If virtually all seminary professors agree with Ehrman, then who are these professors teaching at the ten largest US seminaries? Apparently the only schools that count in Ehrman's analysis of modern seminaries are the ones that already agree with him. It is not so difficult to prove your views are mainstream when you get to decide what is mainstream.[8]

Fact: Plenty of credible scholars have looked at the same arguments your professor may be making and arrived at far different conclusions. You are not as alone as some would have you think.

But their bullying tactics wield a distinct psychological edge over the nineteen-year-old business or nursing majors who only came into this classroom to round out their electives or (in some cases, at some schools) fulfill a course requirement.

How about this: What if we lay down the broad brushes for a second and try a finer approach? Why don't we let a full, firsthand look at the data and a fair representation of the wide scope of opinions help determine what a person ought to believe on these subjects, rather than the assumed infallibility of the learned establishment?

Guys like Ehrman are actually being cleverly contradictory when they dismiss those in the academy whose careful research has led them to trust the biblical record. On the one hand, they say that logic and evidence are the only things that should count—let the best arguments win. But then they suggest there's really no argument to be had, that anyone who disagrees with them is shamelessly biased, and that scholars of their persuasion are the only ones looking at the evidence objectively.[9]

You can agree with *them*, or you can be wrong.

You can be *right*, or you can be bullheaded and backward. Which will it be?

Be sure to pick up on this kind of dismissiveness. It's code for their trying to outflank your competing view, based on nothing other than their opinion.

You've Gotta Have Faith

Finally, *they reinforce the view that faith is at odds with reason.* Much of their appeal depends on the common misunderstanding of what *faith* means—even what it means to many people who have been brought up in the church.

Most people in our culture choose to pocket away the concept of *faith* as a mere personal preference, neither expecting nor requiring it to be grounded in reason, logic, and historical realities. Faith is just something you accept. It doesn't need to be burdened with making rational sense. It just . . .

Is.

Because I *believe* it to be.

The church in large part has become fairly complicit with this misconception. The idea of seeking to support Christian belief with left-brain analysis is seen as suspect at worst, unnecessary at best. Church is a place for us to feel, to move, to act, to sing, not so much to connect the dots between faith and intellect. Bring in too much thinking and theology at a high enough level, and you're doing more the work of the seminary than the local congregation. That's how a lot of believers see it, whether they'll come right out and say it or not.

Faith, however, does not need to be blind. Believing in Christ and accepting the Bible as his true Word is not automatic anti-intellectualism. The Bible doesn't ask us to adopt a *BLIND faith* but a *REASONED faith*—a faith that can honestly ask the hard questions and then go out in search of real, measurable, credible answers.

Did you get that? You sure?

If we've caught your mind wandering, you're forgiven. It's OK. But please come back and pay attention to this point. This is a no-skim zone. Crucially important.

Reasoned faith is a good thing. An attainable thing.

Paul the apostle sure thought so. When he made his case to the Corinthians for the reliability of Jesus' resurrection, he didn't tell them to accept this key doctrine of the church just because he said so. He first referred to written documentation:

"That Christ died for our sins *according to the Scriptures*, that He was buried, that He was raised on the third day *according to the Scriptures*" (1 Cor. 15:3–4, italics added).

Then Paul backed up his claim with eyewitness testimony, saying that Jesus "appeared to Cephas, then to the Twelve. Then He appeared to over 500 brothers at one time; most of them are still alive" (vv. 5–6).

He even went further than that. Paul conceded that if his assertions about the resurrection of Christ didn't hold water, "then our proclamation is without foundation, and so is your faith" (v. 14). In other words, *If you can give me no proof whatsoever that Jesus did what he said he did, then you really have no reason to believe in him.*

How's that for giving verifiable proof a seat at the faith table?

That's why Paul's comment that "most" of the eyewitnesses to Jesus' life, death, and resurrection were "still alive" is so impressive. It's one thing for him to say the risen Christ was seen by a bunch of people who could never be confronted or challenged to their face, whose story could never be interviewed for inconsistencies. It's quite another to dare someone to go find somebody who was actually there: Ask them whatever you want! See if they don't tell you the same thing! Paul wasn't afraid of people following up the evidence. In fact, he *encouraged* this kind of historical investigation.

The Bible was written with the assumption that we are the rational and spiritual beings God made us to be, giving us the created dignity of marrying our belief with reason. Christian faith is true not only because we really want to believe it but also because the truth it believes is the most plausible of all explanations.

Faith *is* reasonable—whether they want you to know it or not.

Authors, speakers, and professors like Bart Ehrman are banking on the assumption that if you find their appeals to reason stimulating—which we hope you do—you won't feel like you can bring your faith along when you go exploring out there. They want you to believe that faith can only play within safe, churchy cloisters where it doesn't need to validate itself against anything *other* than itself. They've created an artificial, scholarly boundary beyond which faith is not strong enough to travel, where it surely will be torn to shreds in the harsh outposts of reality. If you want to go out into the raw, intellectual elements where they're going (and what choice do you really *have* since they'll be giving you a letter grade for it?), you'll need to leave your faith behind, someplace safe.

Our main contention with the critics of Christianity is not that they're making historical accusations against orthodox Christian faith. That's fine. Our problem is that their arguments are simply not the best ones, the most likely ones, the most *reasonable* ones. And yet their skeptical views are allowed to absorb nearly all the oxygen in the average classroom discussion, if not every breath of it.

Faith and reason—even the presence of tough, legitimate questions—can all be friends on the side of authentic Christianity. And any religion professor who isn't willing to accommodate a believer's right to explore truth in the same fields of study as everyone else is surely hiding some insecurity somewhere.

Coming Up

No one—conservative or liberal, Christian or agnostic—can prove the Bible is true (or not true) with 100 percent certainty. To say otherwise is to raise a false standard on both sides. The process of tracing a historical path that stretches back more than two thousand years is far too ancient and complex to turn every question into an open-and-shut case . . . not just on the Bible but on *anything* with such an advanced age attached to it. There's no CSI lab in the world where all debate on these matters can be sewn up in sixty minutes of prime-time police work.

But there are *reasonable* answers to be had that consistently correspond to the beliefs of Christian faith.

And if someone like Bart Ehrman can package these scholarly topics on a national bestseller scale with such skill and persuasion for a skeptical audience, there's no reason why someone like you shouldn't enjoy the same kind of accessible treatment to the same material from a solidly Christian viewpoint. That's why we've written this book. And that's what we hope you'll come away with.

You're likely doing a lot of important things in your spiritual life—reading your Bible, praying, participating in your church, serving in ministry, guarding your heart, striving for purity, doing your best work every day as a steward of your gifts and talents and resources. But gaining a grasp on the historical defense of Christianity is important too. And believe it or not, it's a skill you can pursue with the same burst of spiritual zeal as all the other things that make following Christ such an adventurous lifestyle.

So with this goal in sight, we invite you into a rugged treatment of the harder stuff—the headier stuff—knowing you can
take it, and knowing you'll feel a lot more capable of holding
your own next time the tough questions start flying. Questions
like . . .

- Was Christianity just made up?
- Is the Bible full of irresolvable contradictions?
- Is God incapable of keeping us from suffering?
- What gives the Bible any authority or credibility?
- How can we know what it says if we don't have any
  originals?
- Have the biblical documents been forged to look more
  authentic?
- Why weren't other books included that were just as
  valuable?

How'd you like not to be afraid of answering stuff like that,
or at least be able to spot some of the subtler holes in a skeptical
argument, whether it lands on your school desk, sparks a discussion in your dorm room, or lies strewn about the dark alleys of
your own doubts?

Wouldn't you like that?

And wouldn't right now be a good time to get started?

Discussion Questions

1. What are some doubts or critiques you've heard about the Bible and Christianity?
2. What is the difference between blind and reasoned faith?
3. How would you go about pursuing a reasoned faith?

2

Is God There?
Does God Care?

Then Why Can't He Do Any Better than This?

The God I once believed in was a God who was active in the world. He saved Israelites from slavery; he sent Jesus for the salvation of the world; he answered prayer; he intervened on behalf of his people when they were in desperate need; he was actively involved in my life. But I can't believe in that God anymore, because from what I now see around the world, he doesn't intervene.
—BART EHRMAN[1]

Just because you can't see or imagine a good reason why God might allow something to happen doesn't mean there can't be one. Again we see lurking within this supposed hard-nosed skepticism an enormous faith in one's own cognitive faculties. If our minds can't plumb the depths of the universe for good answers to suffering, well, then, there can't be any! This is blind faith of a high order.
—TIM KELLER[2]

OK, let's jump right into a little game of philosophical honesty.

Before we delve more deeply into the hard evidence that supports a Christian view of the Bible, we want to show you the importance of thinking all the way through what a person is saying, not just doing a quick scan of the top layer and letting it go at that.

When you walk into a college class on religion, biblical history, or any of the more philosophical subjects, it likely is the case that the professor has a skeptical perspective. Maybe that attracts you. Maybe that offends you. Maybe that frightens you. Maybe you just don't want to think about it. But whether you face a professor whose declared agenda is to separate you from your Christian faith or one who is more or less objectively presenting the information without really caring what you do about it, you cannot afford to blank-slate your brain and take everything in at face value.

This is not accounting or chemistry, where a debit is always a debit, an acid always an acid. In this class (and in many others), you need a shovel, not a wheelbarrow. You need to dig and look and filter and examine, not just pick up the load you're given and haul it back to your apartment.

Your instructor may be a recent doctoral grad who's just been itching for this chance—a fresh batch of students on whom to let loose the value of his or her ideas. It may be a tenured professor who is trotting out the same old syllabus for the millionth time. It may be a serious, devoted scholar who's deeply engaged in the field, who'll gladly meet you over coffee to discuss matters further, who truly believes he's shaping a finer breed of thinkers for the next generation.

Only rarely will you look up from your desk to find a professor whose stances are in keeping with what you've been taught to be true about life, about God, and about the Bible. So part of your task as a student (or anybody who's still wanting to learn) is to listen for what's really being said, not just write down what they're saying. You need to follow their statements around and over and through until—like the various wires and cables that snake behind your television—you find the one that actually plugs into the wall.

We're going to practice some of this right now. Ready?

Bart Ehrman says one reason for not believing in God is because of the way he's been reported to "exterminate" people if he "disapproves of how they behave."[3] He also writes, speaking more personally, "I came to believe that there is not a God who is intent on roasting innocent children and others in hell because they didn't happen to accept a certain religious creed."[4]

Now most of us would admit, when we hear things like this, we've pondered some of these same questions ourselves. *Is* there really a God? If so, is it fair for him to make a person's belief in Jesus Christ the one and only pass/fail determiner of their eternal destiny? Shouldn't other contributing factors, other extenuating circumstances also be given weight? Shouldn't God take into account that some people live in countries that are saturated with the gospel while others are rarely if ever exposed to anything except the religious beliefs (or lack thereof) in their own family and culture? How are they supposed to know what

God wants and expects of them? And why should they go to hell for not knowing?

Admittedly, these are fair questions, deserving of much more than pat answers. But for our purposes right now, let's drill a bit deeper into what the Ehrmans of this world are saying and ask ourselves: What's at the bottom of his statement? What are they really saying when they call God out for what he's doing, when they challenge what they perceive to be the way God operates?

Here it is: *God, you cannot be good.*

You shouldn't do it like this.

You should know better.

If you're real (and that's a big IF), you are seriously not handling things right.

Well . . . if what God is doing is wrong, how do we know that? How can we judge his actions to be cruel and immoral? What standard do we use to measure the rightness or wrongness of his behavior? Or of *anyone's* behavior? If there's no God, if there's no Word, no truth, then what makes someone who busts out your windshield any more wrong than if they wash your car or buy you a tank of gas? Without something or someone, somewhere in the universe, to frame our existence in such a way that certain actions are good and others are evil, on what grounds do we decide which is which?

We know how the *biblical* worldview answers this question. But what about theirs? How does *their* worldview deal with it? For them, if there is no mind or Creator behind our existence, then we're just a conglomeration of atoms. There is no god, good or bad.

So they're asking us to believe that these skin cells and blood vessels and brain matter and bone fragments somehow got together—along with all the other material components of our world—and hashed out a code of morality for ourselves. They decided helping was good, hurting was bad. Serving was noble, stealing was wrong. But if we are no more than accidental beings with no Creator to whom we are accountable, then this play-nice morality goes against our essence as individuals. There is simply no rational space within this worldview for people being nice to one another. Why should we be good to one another (whatever "good" means) if we are competitors in an ongoing struggle where the only rule is that we must survive? Unless . . .

Unless, something in our created nature has been marked from birth with a conscience, a moral compass, an inspired indicator that says love and kindness and compassion are a sacred good. Unless there is a created soul tied to God that points our best instincts and sensitivities to the fact that we are created for relationships to others and to a Creator. And our capacity for good is a direct reflection of God's capacity for good.

- So to claim that God isn't treating us right is to say God is wrong.
- And to say God is wrong is to say we know right *from* wrong.
- To make this claim is to say we possess a working conscience.
- And a moral conscience comes from a moral Creator.
- So it actually all testifies to a God who is real and has a standard of morality.

See, you just need to be careful, listening, thinking—because like we said, we all wonder about these things at times. How, for example, can a world that seems so messed up be overseen by a God who knows what he's doing or cares how we're affected by the fallout? It sounds logical to ask that. And if your name was called in class to try offering a rebuttal, to hazard an explanation for why your God and these observations can exist in the same universe, you might not be able to come up with one. You might just choose to believe what they say by default.

That's because to express doubt can sound subtly like the truth when it's fashioned to speak the language of our heart and of our common experience. And that's why digging for the deeper meaning of what's being said is such a vital skill and exercise. That's why it pays to approach these statements with such an active radar of intellectual investigation.

Because our faith *truly is* capable of clinging to reason.

Even within dilemma, tension, and mystery.

Like, for example, the mystery of suffering.

Do we understand why God permits suffering and hardship in our lives? No, not entirely. If he loves us, if he's good, if he cares for us like a father, if he protects us like a shepherd, why would he not exert all his professed power to prevent us from enduring what so often appears to be senseless tragedy? Why would he not choose to spare us and our world from facing such desperate conditions, unending turmoil, acts of obvious evil?

Again, these are good questions. And no one on either side of the philosophical spectrum has the one, slam-dunk, final *Jeopardy* answer for them—not on this side of heaven. Yes, this discussion is filled with imponderable elements, even with the presence of helpful truths, insights, and principles from the Bible. *But to come away believing there is no God since God does not appear good (as we define good) assumes an absolute moral framework which, if God were absent, would not be there at all.*

Underline that. Think about it.

Notice why this observation about suffering, when used as a means of refuting God's goodness or his existence, is a *self-contradicting* or *self-defeating* statement. The same thing it argues against, it also defends. Any person is free to rail all day long about why pain and hunger and death and disease shouldn't be here. Fine. But they cannot legitimately springboard from there to conclude that *God* can't be here. That's a work-around of their own argument.

How Do *You* Know?

The only way someone can *reasonably* determine that suffering and evil should not exist in God's world, and therefore God himself cannot even exist in it, is to possess a "God's-eye view" of the entire situation. If they were to know everything God knows and still not be able to locate an adequate answer to their complaint, only then could they back up such a statement.

We like the way author and pastor Tim Keller refreshes an illustration first advanced by well-known philosopher Alvin Plantinga:

> If you look into your pup tent for a St. Bernard,
> and you don't see one, it is reasonable to
> assume that there is no St. Bernard in your

tent. But if you look into your pup tent for a
"no-see-um" (an extremely small insect with
a bite out of all proportion to its size) and you
don't see any, it is not reasonable to assume
they aren't there. Because, after all, no one can
see 'em. Many assume that if there were good
reasons for the existence of evil, they would be
accessible to our minds, more like St. Bernards
than like no-see-ums, but why should that be
the case?[5]

Yes. Why?

(*Why?* by the way, is often a good question to ask when a
statement you're hearing, despite its convincing hint at sound
reason, still doesn't seem to add up. Maybe you should wonder:
Why doesn't it?)

As much as we may wish to know everything that occupies
the mind of God, surely we see the gap involved here. We can
hardly make our beds, much less make a leaf or a panda bear or
a supernova. We couldn't handle what's in the mind of God. We
couldn't respond to all the things it exposed to us. And even if
we could, the reality is we simply *cannot* know what God knows,
any more than a bird that's fallen out of its nest can know that
the reason you're causing it such anguish and discomfort is only
to transport it back to safety. The Bible *reasonably* tells us to
accept the fact that an infinite God cannot be fully understood
by finite human beings. Because if we could, he wouldn't be
what?—God.

Therefore, we're left with a measure of mystery. Which we
don't like very much. But as limited as we naturally are in our

understanding—with thoughts that weigh next to nothing on a God-size scale—we can only observe these things and see how they appear from our perspective. We can't declare with certainty how they actually are from his. We simply have no way of knowing *all* God's reasons for why he permits suffering as a part of earthly life. Nobody can. And everybody knows it!

Thankfully, he has revealed *some* of his reasons to us, which are helpful and instructive (and which, we can say, he wasn't required to do). But our knowledge is still partial—so partial, in fact, that not only are we acting above our pay grade to accuse God of treating us wrongly, we actually don't know how much worse our suffering could be if not for God's mercy and control. What if we knew the extent of trouble and tragedy he had *prevented* us from experiencing? Would we still consider him cruel? And who knows—what if we might actually like it a lot *less* if he gave us everything we wanted with no hardship or difficulty? Plenty of observations from our own experience prove that having a carefree life is not the secret sauce of happiness.

Ehrman himself agrees that suffering is a real-world concept we cannot completely comprehend. "At the end of the day, one would have to say that the answer is a mystery."[6] And yet he still insists that if *he* can't understand it, if *he* can't figure it out, then there must not be a satisfactory theological explanation for it.

But that only makes sense if he's as smart as God.

And that's a burden none of our shoulders can carry.

Sufferin' Succotash

This little human limitation hasn't kept Bart Ehrman from trying to go there, however. He surveyed all the various books and genres of the Bible in hopes of cataloging all the rationales for suffering that are expressed in Scripture. *Maybe*, he thought, *if he could locate the entire toolbox, he could better understand why God pulls out a particular lightning bolt at one time and not at another.* In the end he arrived at a broad summary of five possibilities. (These are adapted from his book *God's Problem*.)

1. *Suffering comes from God as punishment against sin.* He calls this the "classical view." Like a spanking.

2. *Suffering is the result of human beings sinning against other human beings.* God has given us free will, the ability to make independent decisions, and this freedom can sometimes result in actions that are damaging to ourselves or others.

3. *Suffering is redemptive.* God accomplishes a perceived or actual good through the vehicle of suffering that apparently would not have been possible without it. Ehrman says, by way of personal example, that becoming sick one year as a teenager and being held out of a sports season proved redemptive in his life because the idle time indirectly laid the foundation for his career in academic research. Things like that.

4. *Suffering is a test of faith.* God uses suffering to reveal who will serve him and believe in him no matter their circumstances.

5. *Suffering is mysterious.* The catchall. God doesn't always give us the exact reason we suffer. He just expects us to trust him, to be content with knowing *he* knows, even if we don't.

The problem with this list is not the list (which is actually a pretty good one). The problem is that having a nice, numbered grid of possible choices doesn't even begin to ascertain God's much larger purposes in either imposing or allowing suffering into our lives. Not to mention that this list limits God to only one reason for our suffering, when there may be a combination of reasons. God is not bound by any list, nor is he under orders to treat every person or every problem in the same way. We don't figure out his reasons by trying to hack into God's flow chart of if-then scenarios.

Think of it this way: A basketball coach could call a time-out for any number of reasons at any different point in a ball game. He might see a flaw in the opponent's defense, for example, that he thinks his team could exploit with a hastily designed play. He might want to stop a flurry of momentum or a hot hand by one of the opposing players. He might use it to try icing a free-throw shooter. He might use it to stop the clock near the end of the half or regulation. He might use it to force an instant-replay review of a questionable call by the officials.

That's six different options right there. Easy. And they're all determined not by fixed logarithms but by the flow of the game, the nature of the opponent, the time left on the shot clock or the game clock—any of these factors and many others could dictate his purpose in asking for a stoppage in play. Plus it's all dictated by the coach's unique, personal knowledge of his players, his awareness of what each of them can do, what makes them perform best, what puts them in the best position to win the game.

Why must God's decisions be any different?

Is he bound to use suffering the same way in your life as in your parents' lives—or the same way every time in your *own* life? Pain may arise from a particular set of circumstances here, another set of circumstances there. It may occur with chronic regularity, or it may blindside you out of nowhere. It may be long-term or short-term. It may be obvious; it may be mysterious. But there's no reason for saying that any of these purposes (and more) cannot exist under the omniscient watch of God's wisdom and knowledge—and still square with his goodness, not as *we* define *goodness* but as *he* does. As God.

Some people want to use the Bible to paint him into a corner—to analyze him like a bug under a magnifying glass, to pit his statements and past actions against each other, presenting them as contradictions. But when the various writers and recorders of Scripture spoke on the subject of suffering, they weren't making blanket statements of how it should always be interpreted. Read the Bible as a whole document, and you'll see the multitasking nature of God's work in the world and in our lives, even in cases of distress and difficulty.

The book of Job (to cite the most obvious example) is a classic, forty-two-chapter rebuttal against the notion that painful circumstances in a person's life are always the equivalent of getting a whipping. People tend to think that. "What did I do to deserve this?" But the Bible says Job was "a man of perfect integrity, who feared God and turned away from evil" (Job 1:1), and yet "his suffering was very intense" (Job 2:13). Clearly some other reason was behind this.

Jesus, in the New Testament, specifically challenged this same faulty preconception in his disciples. Seeing a blind man along the road, they asked aloud whose sin was to blame for this guy's sad situation. But Jesus answered, "Neither this man nor his parents sinned. This came about so that God's works might be displayed in him" (John 9:3).

At other times, however, Jesus would say yes, one reason for suffering is as a direct result of human rebellion and disobedience. He once said to a lame man, moments after curing him, "Do not sin anymore, so that something worse doesn't happen to you" (John 5:14). But when responding to a report that said Jews were being murdered by the Roman authorities, he asked, "Do you think that these Galileans were more sinful than all Galileans because they suffered these things?" (Luke 13:2). No.

Jesus wasn't contradicting himself; he was just saying that God has his reasons. *Lots* of reasons. And the fact that they're not always the same across the board, that he applies them in his own wise way, is not tantamount to saying God is wishy-washy or inconsistent, unjust or unaware (or even nonexistent!). He treats us all individually, uniquely, knowing us the way he does—knowing *everything* the way he does.

Let's be honest, though. Most people's problem with any of these rationales for suffering is not that they're impossible to understand or appear contradictory in Scripture. The problem is that they don't *like* them. And the ultimate test for the Bible's truthfulness can never just be based on whether or not a person *likes* what it says. When people already know that the answers they want to find don't exist in real life, and yet those answers are the only ones they're willing to accept, then they're not actually hunting for truth anymore with an open, receptive, inquisitive mind. They're being doubtful skeptics.

Being the kind of skeptic who has already determined where they will land is not being as truly critical and discerning as they claim.

Where Life and Mystery Meet

People want God to live inside their preapproved boxes. They want God and life to be predictable, able to be pulled out and scrutinized and completely buttoned up, like a math problem. They don't want to live with this level of mystery, of not knowing. "If in the end," Ehrman writes, "the question is resolved by saying it is a mystery, then it is no longer an answer. It is an admission that there is no answer."[7]

Hmm.

How surprising that someone like him, an agnostic—meaning he highly doubts whether or not God exists or at least can't say for sure—will not allow Christians equal permission to attribute mystery to God's ways. Your professor may hold this same kind of agnostic view. And when he claims the Bible is insufficient in providing an explanation for evil, he considers his statement a bold stroke of intellectual superiority. A nonbelieving knockout punch. Yet for us to say we're not always privy to what God is doing or what he's allowing through the various mysteries of human suffering is deemed a cop-out.

He can say it; we can't.

The fact is, suffering and evil do leave behind elements of mystery *no matter what perspective or worldview a person adopts*. And while this reality requires us to share space in life with some unknowns and unanswered questions—guests we really didn't want invited to the party—our dislike or discomfort with their presence doesn't mean they can't still walk off with some of our punch and cookies.

The skeptics say God *must* produce better answers than he's given us so far. He *must* make this easier for us to handle and understand. If he's there, if he exists, he *owes* us more satisfying rationales than he's given us for what's going on.

Explain yourself!

But we would counter with this: *God's incarnation in Christ has already done his explaining for him.* When he sent his Son to suffer, he made the boldest statement of all about suffering.

Even if Christ's coming doesn't answer every one of our specific questions, the Bible does say that Jesus entered our world and suffered alongside his people, "becoming obedient to the point of death—even to death on a cross" (Phil. 2:8). "For we do not have a high priest who is unable to sympathize with our weaknesses, but One who has been tested in every way as we are" (Heb. 4:15)—"despised and rejected by men, a man of suffering" (Isa. 53:3).

God in his providence and mysterious love may not always choose to *explain*. But he has expressly chosen to *care*. And while he may not always satisfy us with full-service answers, he has promised and proven, again and again, that he can satisfy his people with fullness of joy, even in the midst of what appears to be unbearable or unjust suffering.

Cue the words of Alvin Plantinga:

> It would be easy to see God as remote and
> detached, permitting all these evils, himself
> untouched, in order to achieve ends that are

no doubt exalted but have little to do with us,
and little power to assuage our griefs. It would
be easy to see him as cold and unfeeling—or if
loving, then such that his love for us has little
to do with our perception of our own welfare.
But God, as Christians see him, is neither
remote nor detached. His aims and goals may
be beyond our ken and may require our suffering, but he is himself prepared to accept much
greater suffering in the pursuit of those ends.[8]

In the final analysis, as Alister McGrath says, "A willingness
to live with irresolvable questions is a mark of intellectual matu-
rity, not a matter of logical nonsense."[9] The incarnation may
not fully explain to human satisfaction the *theoretical* problem of
evil, but it does provide God's powerful and personal response
to the *existential* problem of evil—to the experiences we undergo
as people.

And if someone cannot be satisfied with the heaven-forsaken
lengths to which God has gone to minister to human need, they
obviously wouldn't be satisfied even if a man came back from the
dead to prove it.

Root Issues

Most of people's doubts about God in relation to suffering
stem from two taproots: (1) a refusal to see God as having divine
rights over his creation, and (2) a minimization of the extent of
human rebellion against our Creator.

Admittedly, something within each of us wants to buck at the message behind these truths. We don't want a boss. We don't want to be accountable to God. We don't want to think of ourselves as evil, sinful, wicked, bad. But if people want to deal objectively with God's "problems" in the area of suffering, they must approach them with more than just what they feel and want. They must be willing to back down from their opposing belief systems for a moment and come meet the Bible on an even playing field.

Actually, these are the ground rules for any kind of theoretical debate. Imagine, for example, someone is arguing their case with you about the legitimacy of evolution. If the only brand of responses you can offer starts with words like, "That's not what the Bible says," you won't get very far in advancing your positions. This person most likely couldn't care less what the Bible says. He gives it little to no authority to speak into this discussion. And your insistence on keeping the Bible front and center not only fails to persuade the other person but also keeps you from listening to what he's really saying.

No, in order to understand why someone believes strongly in naturalistic, evolutionary theory, you must hypothetically suspend your belief in God for the time being and engage the other's worldview on *its* terms, not your own. You must play initially on *its* field, with *its* rulebook, exposing its inconsistencies by addressing its *own* issues within its *own* camp, beginning with *those* presuppositions and givens, not yours.

This is where most skeptical arguments falter. They want to rant against the biblical view of suffering, for example, without showing us—based on what the *Bible* says—why we shouldn't reach the conclusions we do, why we're being inconsistent in our thinking. They just basically say, "That's not what I believe." Well, that's fine if all they want to do is feel good about their own opinions. But if they expect to have any chance of changing our minds, they need to blast some holes in the foundational givens of Scripture and show why these can't be right or trusted. Otherwise, they're just lobbing smoke bombs from a careful distance.

Let us show you how this works with the two main points of this section:

Root 1—God has no right to judge or punish.

We understand why this doctrine is among the most offensive of all Christian teachings. We know what makes hell an unpopular sermon topic. But if God is God, as the Bible clearly asserts, then he doesn't need anybody's permission to do anything he wants. We may not *like* that. But if someone wants to challenge the biblical truth that God is God and is therefore entitled to banish a soul to hell, for example, we need to hear them doing more than just standing over there and expressing their hot, personal disdain for it. *Show us, sir, from what the Bible teaches, why God's actions must meet with your and our approval.*

Tim Keller writes of a discussion he had with a woman who shared this type of outrage at God's entitled role as judge. He asked if she was equally offended by the idea of God being forgiving and merciful. *Of course not.* And yet in some corners of the world, that's exactly how people feel. Secular Westerners like us, Keller explained, almost inherently recoil at the Christian doctrine of hell, and yet we generally find the Bible's teachings on forgiveness and turning the other cheek to be quite appealing. Traditional societies, however, tend to have a lot less problem accepting the idea of God's judgment than they do the biblical notion of mercy. The whole idea of releasing a debt seems abhorrent to them, unthinkable, senseless—the same kind of reaction we may feel when we hear about lakes of fire and eternal gnashing of teeth. They are "offended" by a forgiving God, just as we are conditioned to take more natural offense at his judgment and his justice. Keller concluded by saying to the woman, "Why should cultural sensibilities be the final court in which to judge whether Christianity is valid?"[10]

Have you ever thought of it that way? What gives twenty-first-century American poll results the final call on what's acceptable about God's nature and character? How dare he not check with us first? But if God is God—that's the biblical position—what makes him wrong to choose his own actions?

Root 2—The biblical doctrine of sin and the fall.

If someone underestimates the effects of this one reality on human existence, he or she will never succeed at delving fully into these "problem" areas with the Bible.

In a general sense all suffering is rooted in rebellion against God. There was no suffering of any kind in the paradise he created, the garden of Eden in which he placed the first man and woman. But when they sinned, the perfection of God's created order twisted into a downward spiral. And each successive generation, each person who's ever lived—us!—we're all part of the rebellion. We don't *deserve* free and easy lives. (A hard statement, yes, but consistent with a biblical worldview.) In a world like ours, hostile and indifferent toward God, why should we expect *not* to quake with the painful results of both our cosmic and individual sin?

Most folks limit their understanding of evil to the horizontal level—people harming other people. The Bible, however, affirms that even the person-on-person, relational nature of evil and suffering is in essence a vertical rebellion against God, his authority, his principles, and his rule. When King David, reeling in shame from his acts of adultery and murder, said to God, "Against You—You alone—I have sinned and done this evil in Your sight" (Ps. 51:4), he was painfully experiencing a deep, biblical truth. We not only inflict damage on *others* when we lie to them, steal from them, abuse them, mistreat them. We are ultimately offending a holy and righteous God.

The Bible says, "All have sinned and fall short of the glory of God" (Rom. 3:23), that we were born with a nature that resists him. And we needn't look back any further than the last twenty-four hours to see the Bible come to life on this subject—in *your* life, in *our* lives. Obeying him is tough on us. Sinning, by contrast, is a piece of cake. With ice cream. We are hard-wired to ignore him, to overrule him, to do whatever we want. And we do it without even stopping to realize that the effort required to sin against him is only ours because he gave it to us—the mind, the muscles, this involuntarily breathing, blood-pumping apparatus with which we defy him.

So when seen from this most basic of biblical views—the doctrine of sin and the fall—the real mystery is not that we suffer. The mystery is that he's ever let us enjoy any blessing at all: the simple pleasure of a smile, a laugh, a walk in the grass, the strength for an afternoon workout, the warmth of family and friends. Perhaps from this perspective we might actually ponder the "problem of good"—why any of us should experience the abundant, though often unnoticed, presence of mercy and provision in our daily lives.

It can only be by the grace—the *common grace*—of God.

If someone desires to challenge him on the "suffering and evil" plank in his platform, they need to show us where this preconception comes from. If they believe we are somehow owed his goodness and blessing, and that every form of suffering is tantamount to God's refusal to grant us what we so self-evidently deserve (if he's even there to grant it), they need to explain why this logically follows what we believe to be true about human nature.

Many people wish to declare God immoral for making us put up with evil and suffering. But here's the important part to remember: they only succeed at showing us why they *feel* that way, not why it *is* that way. They try debunking the Bible by shooting at it with their own arguments, hoping we'll accept their claims because of our shared personal suspicions and experiences. Yet all the while, the Bible stands consistent, even if misunderstood, misrepresented, and misjudged. And God stands absolved.

Why do bad things happen to good people? The Bible's answer is: *They don't.* While obviously gradients of good distinguish one person from another—a Hitler from a Mother Teresa, for example—the Bible teaches that all of us, in our own way, have slapped God in the face, shaken our defiant fist toward heaven, and demonstrated our self-styled intention to do things our own way. So if by suffering we are not getting what we deserve, it is only that we actually deserve far worse.

The Homesick Skeptic

We go back to our opening point: Without the existence of God, no one has any grounds for making these moral judgments against him. Sure, they can dispute and disagree with us on everything else from that point forward. But whenever we engage in an ethical debate of any sort, we are proving by the nature of our conversation that we're in the presence of God. That's just an unavoidable consequence of reason. Without God, right and wrong come with no dictionary definitions.

God is here. Period.

So don't let anyone make you feel that being intellectually thoughtful means accepting that God is not real.

But you can certainly agree with others wholeheartedly on one thing: *The harsh, hurting reality we feel within ourselves and see in the world around us is not the way life should be.* Obviously something has gone horribly wrong. No, the problem is not with *God*, but yes, there's still a problem.

And yet perhaps what people feel by discounting God and his goodness is less an inborn frustration or complaint and more of a hidden longing, placed there by the one who planted his own image into the body and soul of every person he created. Perhaps, as Alister McGrath has written, this dilemma is "a matter of the heart, rather than the head." "Where does this deep-seated intuition that suffering and pain are not right come from? . . . What if this intuition points to something deeper—something built into us that reflects our true nature and identity? What if this revulsion against suffering and pain is a reminder of paradise, on one hand, and an anticipation of the New Jerusalem on the other?"[11]

Perhaps it's the cry of the human spirit for God.

The world people think we can create with enough human effort—a world without poverty, without AIDS, with lots of goodwill and cooperation all around—has actually been created already by the only one capable of creating it. And he's done it despite the human pride, human lust, and human rejection of his divine authority that's invited all this suffering into our lives to start with.

Here's how the Bible describes what's coming: Jesus Christ, who chose to die for us "while we were still sinners" (Rom. 5:8), has gone away to "prepare a place" for his people (John 14:2)—"a new heaven and a new earth" where he will "wipe away every tear," where "death will no longer exist," and where "grief, crying, and pain" will never darken our door again. The old experiences of suffering and evil will represent "the previous things," and they will all "have passed away" (Rev. 21:1, 4). And since eternal paradise is what everyone hopes for, perhaps this sense that even the skeptics feel about the brokenness of our current condition is in some way pointing all of us toward a day when God *will* make all things right.

We join people, of course, in wanting to make our present world as peaceful, productive, and compassionate as possible. But no matter how hard we try, it can never outgrow what it is—a home to self-willed sinners whose choices, both personal and generational, leave no other alternative than toil and trouble.

Some might say they would say, no, if God does exist, *he* is responsible for the evil in the world, not us—the blood is on *his* hands. But the Bible says the only blood on *God's* hands is the atoning blood of Christ—blood that forgives a believer's sins, heals all our diseases, redeems us from the hell we deserve, and satisfies us with his goodness forever (see Ps. 103:3–5).

The one some blame for all this suffering is the only one who actually has done everything that needed to be done about it.

Discussion Questions

1. What are some examples of pain and suffering in your life?

2. How does a Christian understanding of Jesus' crucifixion help us deal with suffering?

3. If we were to imagine there was no God, what would that imply about suffering and evil?

4. Why can the existence of evil and suffering not disprove God, and how does it actually serve as a powerful argument for the existence of God?

Let's Make a Bible

Who Picked These Books, and Where'd They Come From?

What if the New Testament contained not Jesus' Sermon on the Mount but the Gnostic teachings Jesus delivered to his disciples after his resurrection? What if it contained not the letters of Paul and Peter but the letters of Ptolemy and Barnabas? What if it contained not the Gospels of Matthew, Mark, Luke, and John but the Gospels of Thomas, Philip, Mary, and Nicodemus?
—BART EHRMAN[1]

Ehrman's extensive cataloging of diversity makes for an interesting historical survey but does not prove what he thinks it does, namely that apocryphal books have an equal claim to originality as the books of the New Testament. The only way that the mere existence of diversity could demonstrate such a thing is if there was nothing about the New Testament books to distinguish them from the apocryphal books. But, that is an enormous assumption that is slipped into the argument without being proven.
—MICHAEL KRUGER[2]

The Bible is not only the best-selling book of all time; it is also the best-selling book of the year. Every year. This year. And not just by a little bit but by at least double—probably much more, to tell you the truth—than its nearest competitor in the marketplace. Actual numbers are hard to determine.

Remember, we're talking about people buying a book that most of them already own. (The average American household has four.) Yet even the most conservative estimates on annual Bible sales in the U.S. would place the figure in the neighborhood of twenty-five million copies.[3] And most likely, that only covers about one street in the neighborhood. Add international sales, add giveaways, add ministry purchases, add missionary usage. If God didn't already own the cattle on a thousand hills, think of the royalties.

But while the demand for this product is stratospherically high and showing no signs of slacking off—from now till Jesus comes—most people (even most Christians) are fairly clueless as to why the Bible is comprised of the particular pieces it includes. Why *these* books? Why not others?

Unlike other books that rest on store shelves today and in thumbnail images online, the Bible wasn't dreamed up on a napkin or created with hopes of becoming the next big thing in publishing. It wasn't assembled like an all-star cast for a benefit concert or trotted out with a fancy marketing blitz and media campaign. It wasn't the brainchild of a well-funded investor, sending out invitations to famous contributors, hoping to fill the pages of one grand anthology project with the most important writings known to man.

So did the Bible just evolve? Did it start out with a few selections and keep adding others as good ones came along? Did a literary board weed out new submissions and reject proposals that didn't quite measure up? On what grounds were these particular books accepted, and on what grounds were others sent back to their "nice try" inkwells?

It all seems rather arbitrary and suspicious.

But, no, it's really not. You'll see.

Here's how we'll do it. Since most of the questions that are likely to come up in your classes involve issues surrounding the *New Testament*, we want to focus this chapter on that portion of the Bible. The books that formed what we now know as the *Old Testament*—the Hebrew Scriptures—were mostly established by that time. Jesus and his apostles, based on statements and quoted passages that appear in Scripture, certainly accepted most of these books as authoritative and inspired. Some faith traditions, you're probably aware—Roman Catholics in particular—accept a handful of later, apocryphal books as well. (The word *Apocrypha* indicates something of doubtful authenticity.) But most who consider these extra writings to be helpful and instructive flatly recognize that these books are not on par with the others. There is little to no dispute about the core of the Old Testament we see the New Testament use (Torah, key prophets like Isaiah and Jeremiah, Psalms, Proverbs).

But when we turn to the early time zones of our present age—the days that orbited more directly around the life of Christ and the emergence of the church—we see something else: the organic creation of holy Scripture that would ultimately become the twenty-seven books, Gospels, Acts, letters of the New Testament, and the Revelation.

And yet not surprisingly, we also detect a noticeable uptick in skeptical doubt. But we'll give you a tip-off from the start—the arguments against the New Testament construction are flimsy at best. Its inquisitors work really hard to question the origins and validity of this collection of writings, but the holes in their claims are large and mostly puzzling. That's because defending the composition of the New Testament is a position of total strength, bolstered by all kinds of reasonable evidence. And by the time you've plowed through the pages of this chapter with us, we think you'll see exactly what we're talking about.

Let's dig right in.

Fire Up the Canon

The impression skeptics may leave behind is that the accepted catalog of New Testament books was hammered out in formal church councils during the fourth century AD. (We'll talk more about these councils in chapter 6.) The picture that's painted for you is almost like the awards committee, sorting through applications and essays, picking out those that are worthy of acceptance, then running all their decisions through a metric that plays to the advantage and stated aims of the institution.

Nothing could be further from the truth.

First of all, the whole concept of a *canon* (meaning a group of texts that are recognized as authoritative) was not some legislative wild card dreamed up by a bunch of committee members.

The importance of canon already contained a long history. In fact, by the time of the massive church meetings in the AD 300s, the canon of the New Testament *had already been forming on its own—and had actually been closed to all newcomers—for generations.*

Evidence suggests the early church, whose structure began developing quickly after the ascension of Jesus and the startling events of Pentecost (Acts 2), became immediately aware they were dealing with something huge here when it came to certain writings. Those texts quickly became useful and began to circulate between local churches. Raised on the canon of Jewish Scripture, they began to recognize that this "new covenant" through Christ, which grew out of the "old covenant" of the Jewish people with God, would naturally find its way into a body of written texts. So even as these first-century groups were going about the business of living out their new life in Christ, God was working to inspire and supply them with documents that would house his teaching and story, preserving it for posterity.

In fact, you can watch this process happening yourself as you flip through the pages of your own Bible. The following three examples point to early knowledge among believers that Scripture was blooming before their eyes. Our first selection is from the pen of the apostle Peter, referring to the letters of Paul. Focus hard on the last line: "Regard the patience of our Lord as an opportunity for salvation, just as our dear brother Paul has written to you according to the wisdom given to him. He speaks about these things in all his letters in which there are some matters that are hard to understand. The untaught and unstable twist them to their own destruction, as they also do *with the rest of the Scriptures*" (2 Pet. 3:15–16, emphasis added).

Peter mentions this thought almost in passing, as if no one should be surprised to hear him give voice to the thought—how he was already putting the writings of Paul on a par with the Old Testament Scriptures. Ehrman believes 2 Peter is a forgery, composed by an early second-century writer. (We'll deal with that soon.) But even if someone applies a later date of authorship to this letter, it still shows a canon emerging long before the church councils of the fourth century convened.

Here's another entry, from Paul's first letter to Timothy: "The *Scripture* says: 'Do not muzzle an ox while it is treading out the grain,' and, 'the worker is worthy of his wages'" (1 Tim. 5:18, emphasis added).

Some say this *isn't* Paul talking, and they want to push the date of its writing to around AD 100. But again, set that aside and note what's happening here. A quote from Deuteronomy 25:4 (the muzzled ox part) is paired with what appears to be Luke 10:7—a New Testament citation of the words of Jesus. This gives us another clue in our search for authenticity. First-century Christians were already viewing Luke's Gospel, or at least some sayings of Jesus in it, in the same vein as Old Testament Scripture.

A final example. Peter again: "Dear friends, this is now the second letter I have written to you; in both letters, I want to develop a genuine understanding with a reminder, so that you can remember the words previously spoken *by the holy prophets* and the command of our Lord and Savior *given through your apostles*" (2 Pet. 3:1–2, emphasis added).

"The holy prophets" and the "apostles." Old and New together—right there in the same sentence—showing that early in church history the complete canon was clearly coming together. In fact, by the end of the second century, the church father Irenaeus utilized a set of authoritative apostolic writings comprised of twenty of the eventual twenty-seven books of the New Testament, including a specific listing of the widely accepted four Gospels: Matthew, Mark, Luke, and John.[4] Another ancient document, the Muratorian Canon—most likely the earliest list of authoritative Christian books (around AD 180)—also affirms the four New Testament Gospels as being the only ones recognized as Scripture.[5]

This means the thirteen letters of Paul, in short order with the Gospels and other writings of the apostles, were already being viewed as bearing the equal weight of Scripture. Irenaeus mentions each of Paul's epistles except Philemon, while the Muratorian Canon includes all of them. A measure of debate would continue throughout the coming years on some of the peripheral books (2 Peter, 2 and 3 John, James, and Jude), but the core canon of the New Testament appears to have been consistently sanctioned churchwide by at least the middle of the *second century*—long before any councils had obtained the political wherewithal to force heretical books out.

It wasn't a contest. It never was.

So while certain scholars present the meeting agendas of later centuries as being conniving and conspiratorial in terms of how the Bible was fashioned, the truth doesn't bear this out. The early Christians—due to their deep convictions about the foundational role of the apostles—had long considered the canon of Scripture closed to any writings composed after the deaths of these men. A book known as the Shepherd of Hermas, for example, was rejected by believers as early as the second century, simply because it was "written very recently, in our times."[6] Church leaders in succeeding generations would echo this sentiment, such as Origen, who listed all twenty-seven New Testament books in an early third-century sermon.[7] Another example comes from Dionysius, bishop of Corinth in the middle of the second century, who took pains to distinguish his own letters from what he already called the "Scriptures of the Lord."[8] He, too, believed the canon to be a closed entity with no more writings to be included. In addition, some books touted were explicitly excluded from being included before these councils met. For example, Origen at one point observed that the Gospel of Thomas is not read in the churches.

In sum, the books of the New Testament were recognized (not selected) as cream that had risen to the top, used by churches because they were seen to have unique and special value.

Bottom line: The establishment of the orthodox canon was hardly an "aha!" creation proposed by clever aides and advisors to the church council members of the fourth and later centuries. Actually, *the canon was not even a point of discussion at those meetings*! These gatherings were called for the purpose of clarifying theological issues (like who exactly is Jesus or how to define *Trinity*), and the only reason the canon came up at all was because these books were the ones the church leaders appealed to in defending their various arguments, opinions, and interpretations.

These men didn't converge on the big city to go *make* a Bible; the Bible had already come together long before. Yet the skeptics want you to think a wide number of other books

and gospels—equally valid, bearing equal right to holy writ—
were tossed out of the canon during this time without fair
consideration.

Well, we'll see about that.

Leagues Apart

Among the skeptical arguments you're likely to hear on this
subject is how there's no way to distinguish between the books
that were included in the New Testament and the writings that
were excluded. They claim the choice was like a singing contest
with subjective judges who already knew the ones they wanted
to pick, despite the similar talents and worthiness of all contes-
tants. The truth is, the books regularly cited by skeptics—such
as the ones listed by Ehrman at the beginning of this chapter—
cannot carry a tune in the biblical bucket. No one could have
gotten away with foisting these books on the early believers or
stuffing them into the accepted canon of Scripture.

Since you will hear the same types of claims from others,
let's look at the books Ehrman mentions.

To begin with, wide agreement among scholars tags the
authorship date for each of these so-called competitors somewhere inside the second and third centuries, along with the
offshoot factions of Christianity they typically represented,
such as Gnosticism. (Much more on this subject in chapter 6 as
well.) Unlike all the books of the New Testament canon, these
selections contain no conceptual link with the first century.
Their authors attributed their works to important figures in the
early church, hoping to lend authority to their writing. But no

evidence—none—places any of these documents at the scene of the apostles' lives and ministries.

Here are the kinds of books we're dealing with.

The Letter of Ptolemy

This piece is from a Gnostic author in the second century, probably around AD 150–170. Its writer was committed to a form of Gnosticism that claimed the Old Testament didn't come from God but from an intermediate deity he called the "Demiurge." The author claimed neither to be an original follower of Jesus nor a companion of one. Sound like any of the other New Testament writings you're familiar with? Not hardly. No memory verses here.

The Letter of Barnabas

Composed in the second century by an unknown author, this letter claims to have been written by Paul's bright-hearted companion from his first missionary journey. This popular book was quoted at times in the writings of certain church leaders of the second and third centuries, but no more than your pastor might inject into his sermon a selected line from a book he'd read. Simply because this book was quoted does not mean most early Christians considered it Scripture. In fact, it seems clear most did not.

The Gospel of Thomas

This book is not a Gospel in the pattern of the four Gospels of Scripture. It has no story line, no narrative, no account of Jesus' birth, death, or resurrection. It contains 114 sayings allegedly attributed to Jesus, and though some of them sound like things you might hear in Matthew, Mark, Luke, or John, many of them are strange and bizarre. Broad consensus places its writing in the early to late second century, but it never factored into canonical discussions at any time. In fact, Cyril of Jerusalem specifically warned against reading it in the churches,[9] and Origen characterized it as an apocryphal gospel.[10] The following statement sums it up: "If *Thomas* does represent authentic, original Christianity, then it has left very little historical evidence of that fact."[11]

The Gospel of Philip

Again, this is a Gnostic document, likely written in the third century, long after the time of the apostles. It shows clear dependence on New Testament material and is structured more as a theological catechism for Gnosticism than a historical narrative. The date and content put it far outside the scope of what went for Scripture in the early church.

The Gospel of Mary

Also of Gnostic origin, this book appears to be a development of New Testament material to match the author's own beliefs and has no claim of being based on eyewitness testimony. Written in the second century.

The Gospel of Nicodemus

Hailing from much later—fifth or sixth century—this writing is a fictional account of an interaction between Jesus and

Pontius Pilate as well as Jesus' experiences in hell between his death and resurrection. There are no good reasons for affirming the historical legitimacy of the events it describes and certainly no reason for thinking it belongs in Scripture.

So there you have it. These are some of the most discussed of the "other" gospels. And obviously, little if anything justifies including them within the circle of New Testament Scripture. In fact, an important study by none other than Bruce Metzger— Bart Ehrman's mentor at Princeton—states that the books which in due course would make up the accepted canon were already functioning in an authoritative role *before* they were part of any canonical list. Yet Ehrman and others continue to argue that books like the ones we've just summarized were right up there with the others and could just as easily have made it into our Bibles as the books that actually appear.

The only way to make this appeal seem plausible is not by elevating the obvious weaknesses in these apocryphal writings but by yanking down on the books whose tradition and legacy have spoken loudly from the very beginning in favor of their inclusion in Scripture. Instead of bringing the questionable documents up, they're forced to drag the unquestionable documents down by tactics like questioning their credentials, integrity, and legitimacy; by painting Jesus' disciples as illiterate; and by accusing this whole lot of biblical literature as the result of an elaborate scheme.

Marquee Names

When Bart Ehrman releases a new book, he goes on a nationwide signing and speaking tour, hitting some of the big New York and California media, finding quick reception by the talent scheduler at Comedy Central who love having him on their talk shows. That's what you get when you write mega-best-selling books and can make a good appearance on camera.

But what about when some I. M. Nobody prints up his own scholarly volume through Publish-or-Perish Press—a book that's probably only been read by his mother, his editor, and maybe opened and closed for ten seconds by friends and colleagues who just need to tell him they've looked at it? Do you think the lines of people wanting to meet this author will wrap around the front windows of the bookstore? Do you think Oprah's returning his phone calls?

They want big names. They want big numbers. They want instant attachments to automatic success.

So when the PR-spinning creators of the Bible went looking for possible entries to include—the kind that would really impress the public, the kind that would put Christian belief on the map and force the world to pay attention—who would they want these books to be written by?

Somebody like . . . Mark?

If the early church was going for instant punch and credibility by attributing their Gospels to heavy-hitting authors, why would they pick a guy like him—somebody who couldn't hack the stress and strain on the road with Paul on his first missionary journey, who went squealing home to Mama, and whose desire for a second chance on a second trip created such a rift between major players Paul and Barnabas, they decided to split up and go their separate ways (see Acts 13:2–5, 13; 15:36–39)?

Hello, Mark. How'd you like to write a book for our new Bible?

Never going to happen.

It's well known now, and was well known then, in a tradition that reaches back to the early second century, that much of what Mark reported in his Gospel came from the preaching and eyewitness testimony of Peter. His first chapter records how Jesus called Peter away from his fishing business to follow him (Mark 1:16–18), and the last chapter records an angel telling the women who discovered the empty tomb, "Go, tell His disciples *and Peter*" to come meet up with the risen Christ (Mark 16:7).

How easy would it have been, if name recognition was the objective and if forgery was the plan, to drop Mark's involvement to the level of invisible ghostwriter and put Peter's name up there on the big, glossy book jacket? He was the natural choice. He was well known and highly regarded. He was an instant seller. Why then would tradition select . . . Mark?

Because tradition must know something. Like that Mark was the one who wrote it. Just as Matthew wrote his Gospel. Just as Luke wrote his. John stands alone as the sole Gospel writer who truly brought high-level apostolic ambience to the quartet.

So we assure you, if the intention of the early church was merely to assign names to Gospel documents in hopes of investing them with greater authority, these rather obscure characters from the original crowd would *not* have been given top billing.

Stick to the Story

OK, if they can't really hitch their doubts to that horse, what about this one? Let's say the Gospels were primarily folk literature that was passed down by people with no interest in history, no attachments to the eyewitnesses, and no qualms with changing the traditional teachings of Jesus to fit their own particular purpose.

This theory has bubbled up from a fairly recent development in scholarly study (early twentieth century) called *form criticism*. Form critics have latched onto the oral nature of how information was commonly relayed between people, groups, and families during the early centuries, leaving them to question how reliable the surviving written books could be as a result.

The substantial insights chronicled in *Jesus and the Eyewitnesses* by British scholar Richard Bauckham have shed impressive light on this controversial subject.[12] He argues, for example, that many of the eyewitnesses to Jesus' life, death, and resurrection were still in wide, active circulation during these years, able to function as trusted, authoritative sources and guardians of the tradition—a commonly revered practice and presence in oral societies. Even as advancing age took them away from the living community, the wide range of years in which the early church was populated with some combination of (a) firsthand observers of Christ, (b) elders that sat personally at their feet, and (c) the disciples of those who had heard these accounts of Jesus from an original source stretches well into the second century.[13]

Besides, the zeal of this vibrant, tight-knit, revolutionary church movement alone would have motivated them to cling like glue to what the eyewitnesses had said, like trying to keep intact the tiniest shreds of memory that link you to a departed loved one or to your family back home. These people had a vested stake in keeping these traditions pure and unblemished and would hardly have been militantly motivated to change them or to watch them dissolve away by indifference. Yes, they might retell the accounts with some variation as our gospels shows, but the essence of the stories remained constant.

One of us (Darrell), in a public debate with liberal scholar John Dominic Crossan, listened to his citing of a famous Emory University survey of students about the fickleness of memory in relation to eyewitness events, in this case the space shuttle *Challenger* disaster. I countered by asking if the results might have proved different had the survey been taken with active astronauts rather than with less interested, aloof college students. My point was that people who had actually sat in the spacecraft, who were invested in the program, would likely have come away from this stunning event with much clearer, much less distracted memories of what happened, without being as susceptible to outside persuasion that might cause them to doubt or "misremember" what they saw.

The church had a death-defying interest in maintaining the precise integrity of what Jesus had actually done and said. The vividness, detail, vantage point, and perspective of the Gospels—as we read them today—even the inclusion of many people by name, including a cavalcade of minor characters, all builds a case that this testimony was true and accurate. In the end the extremely high likelihood that these writings contain eyewitness reporting on Jesus' life and ministry means the burden of proof is on the *critic*, not the Bible-believing Christian, to demonstrate with reasonable evidence that the accounts and descriptions written there are *not* historically plausible. Otherwise, the Gospels point to their own reliability.

A Backwoods Illiterate Peasant?

So far we've looked at (1) the literary honesty implied in the choice of lesser-known gospel writers. We've also looked at (2) the bulldog tenacity of eyewitnesses who would have pressed with their last pointer finger muscle to make sure the accurate events and occurrences of Scripture were told accurately the way they happened.

Now we take on another skeptical complaint: *the questionable smarts and capabilities of Jesus' disciples.* As in, how could a couple of ragtag yahoos like Peter and John, pulled in off the street and seashore to be Jesus' closest followers, write the kind of literature we're still pumping out by the millions every month?

That's a cocky kind of comment, don't you think? But listen to what Ehrman calls the apostle Peter: "a backwoods illiterate peasant."[14] (Ouch.) And he uses this one apostle as a test case to cast aspersions on all the others as well, grouping them together as people who couldn't write a memorable line of prose if a steak dinner was on the line, much less write a single word that advertises itself as holy Scripture.

If you ever hear an accusation like this bandied about, keep the following information in mind:

First, *literacy and education were a priority to first-century Jews.*
By the age of six or seven, boys in that culture were expected
to engage in these types of pursuits.[15] Sociologists tell us that
ethnic identity among minorities—even today—leads them to
infuse their traditions hard into their children and families,
making sure their heritage is preserved as a way of life. The
Jews of Roman Palestine were surely no different. And that's not
just projecting our modern mind-sets onto an ancient culture.
The archaeological evidence from Peter's hometown region of
Galilee backs it up. It configures a clear picture of Jewish practice as well as a legal awareness among the community that the
education of their young was of prime concern.

Second, *the disciples' occupations required literacy and knowledge.* The everyday acts of conducting commerce as a merchant
tradesman called for a level of linguistic and cultural engage-
ment. Professor and pastor Ben Witherington adds even more
detail:

> First of all, fishermen were not peasants. They
> often made a good living from the Sea of
> Galilee, as can be seen from the famous and
> large fisherman's house excavated in Bethsaida.
> Secondly, fishermen were businessmen, and
> they had to either have a scribe or be able to
> read and write a bit to deal with tax collectors,
> toll collectors, and other business persons.
> Thirdly, if indeed Jesus had a Matthew/Levi
> and others who were tax collectors as disciples,
> they were indeed literate. . . . In other words, it

is a caricature to suggest that all Jesus' disciples were illiterate peasants.[16]

Third, *the early church movement was cross-cultural.* And Peter was an established leader of this enterprise, meaning he was successfully able to navigate the Greco-Roman settings in which Greek was the main language of both speech and writing. He obviously became a solid oral communicator from the images we see of him in the Bible. And there's no real reason beyond blind speculation to say he wasn't equally capable of expressing himself in letters, especially by the end of his life when he had ministered in these contexts for decades.

Besides, even if this was an issue, the practice of using secretaries for dictation of letters and ideas was a common practice in first-century society. Nothing should have prevented him from getting his words on the page, even on the outside chance that writing wasn't his strong suit.

It is true that this larger culture was largely illiterate (as much as 90 to 95 percent). But Peter, as a tradesman and as an international traveler, in all likelihood was not in that large group. Peter may or may not have been the intellectual equal of Bart Ehrman or your professor. But that doesn't disqualify him from doing what he did and writing what he wrote.

Lying, Cheating Scoundrels

Forgery.

That's ultimately what Bart Ehrman says was taking place when the books of your New Testament were being prepared for widespread circulation. He looks at the evidence and sees no other sound conclusion.

We'll give him this much: he's correct in claiming that forgery was a prevalent issue in the early centuries of our era—much more common than today with our sophisticated ways of telling the difference. But just because this is true doesn't mean you should dismiss all other possibilities and start from an assumption of rampant forgery. It's like saying every married couple living in a culture of divorce is sure to close up shop eventually on their relationship. Or that any student trying to make passing grades in a culture of widespread cheating is incapable of depending on his own hard work as long as old tests are being passed around the dormitory halls.

(You wouldn't do that, would you?)

When forgery is what you're looking for, you can make the suspicions pop up everywhere you look.

Here's what the evidence tells us, however. The early church was aggressive almost to the point of paranoia in making sure no type of funny business was happening with their sacred texts. In general, their tendency was to *reject* rather than *accept* any book whose authorship was in question. The book of Hebrews is actually the exception that proves the rule. The questions that circled even then (as they still do today) about whether or not Paul was the author of Hebrews made it one of their last inclusions in the biblical canon. In the end the church decided it spoke with the consistency and uncommon authority characterizing a work of Scripture, despite the questionable conclusions that remained about who wrote it.

And if Hebrews almost didn't get in, then no Gospel of Thomas or Philip or Mary was getting in. You can bank on that.

But the doubters still entertain and endorse the notion that foul play was afoot. Among the books they call out for particular suspicion are these. Let's mark them as test cases:

Test Case 1: 1 Peter

First Peter shows itself forged (it is claimed) because the author claims Peter witnessed Jesus' suffering (5:1) and because of its use of Babylon as a code word for Rome (5:13), which reflects post-70 AD usage. (The traditional date of 1 Peter's writing is in the early 60s.)

We know, of course, how Peter famously denied Christ three times and ran off into the night weeping with shame and despair. But let's at least say this: he didn't flee at the moment of Jesus' arrest but was obviously in the area where the trial was taking place, albeit at a comfortable distance and without the courage to admit his personal connection as a Christ follower. To refute the wording of 1 Peter 5:1, however, a skeptic would need to define the "sufferings of the Messiah" which Peter claimed to have witnessed as being nothing other than the crucifixion event itself. We'll concede for argument's sake that he may have bailed on that, but he saw enough with his own eyes to know his Lord was in grave danger. He knew Jesus' sufferings firsthand.

As to the Babylon part, it wasn't uncommon in ancient literature (not just the New Testament) to use code language in describing world powers. You see it in the book of Daniel, for example, how he pictures the world's kingdoms as part of his end-time vision. Babylon was part of a chain of evil nations (including Egypt and Assyria) who, like Rome, had cruelly mistreated God's people throughout their history. This metaphor would have communicated instantly with Peter's readers, while subtly veiling the identity of Rome as the place he was talking about. No need to invite more persecution by calling them out by name and letter.

Test Case 2: 2 Peter

Second Peter shows itself forged (some say) because of the notion of delay in Jesus' return (3:8–9), the author's use of language from the book of Jude (3:3–4), and the claim that Paul's letters were equivalent to Scripture (3:15–16). Each of these indicates a later period of writing.

We can take these one at a time: (1) The church was already grappling with the apparent delay of Christ's return, even prior to AD 70 when the Jewish temple was destroyed. (2) As far as his sharing of information with Jude pertaining to the "scoffers" of their day, this would not have been out of character for how Peter associated his ministry with others—like with Mark, for example, as we've seen. And (3) while Paul never claimed outright to be composing words of Scripture, he did say it was *anathema* (a strong rebuke) for people to go around proclaiming a different gospel than the one he had received from God (Gal. 1:6–9).

Besides, other forgeries (including the Gospel of Peter) were written to promote views that veered away from orthodox Christian beliefs. Why would the church need to *forge* a document like 2 Peter if its teaching was "consistent with the church already, and thus they would have no motive to promote it falsely under the name of an apostle?"[17] Second Peter has no divergent agenda. It doesn't refer to doctrinal controversies of the second century. It bears all the earmarks of being included in the canon for a simple yet far less scandalous reason: *Peter actually wrote it.*

Test Case 3: Ephesians

Ephesians shows itself forged (detractors argue) because the style, sentence lengths, vocabulary, and theology are distinct from Paul's other letters.

We could go on, but this is a hair-splitter if ever there was one. Ehrman argues that Ephesians contains 116 words that Paul uses nowhere else in his letters. Yet similar ratios exist in letters like Galatians, which virtually no one denies as Paul's work. Plus, the theological subject matter Paul addresses, unlike that from some of his other writings, was not occasioned by a specific problem in the Ephesian church but was rather meant to be circulated regionally as a presentation of general doctrine.

What do they want Paul's letters to do? All say the same thing? All use the same words? Between the three of us, we've written dozens of books—different lengths, on different subjects, to different audiences. True, you can track tendencies in a person's writing style. But if you performed the same mathematical, comparative analysis on a modern author's breadth of books, you'd probably find equal if not more variety of language than this, especially if they worked with different editors as they composed.

We like how New Testament scholar Mike Licona sums up the situation: "Before jettisoning belief in the traditional authorship of any of the 27, the arguments against it must be reasonably stronger than the arguments for it and be able to withstand the counterarguments. Some like Ehrman appear to take a different approach, assuming that all of the 27 are guilty of false attribution until nearly unimpeachable evidence to the contrary can be presented."[18]

The B–I–B–L–E

It's really not as complicated as skeptical scholars and professors would lead you to assume. Most, if not all, of the New Testament documents were completed by the end of the first century. Though the process that resulted in the twenty-seven books of our canon was not initiated by a think tank or tested in a science lab, the general ground rules for acceptance seemed to be that they were authoritative books and letters (a) written by an apostle or (b) by someone connected with an apostle, and (c) based on eyewitness, verifiable testimony. And when that season of time came and went around AD 100, the book was closed for all practical purposes.

On the other hand, those apocryphal Letter of Ptolemy to Flora-type documents were all written in the second and third centuries or later. And even if they could be magically transported back into the double-digit years of the first millennium, they still don't possess the gravitas to stand on the same platform with the established books of the New Testament.

They never did.

It didn't take a church council to figure that out. It didn't take steel-toed intimidation to kick them out of the canon.

The books of the biblical canon showed themselves to be special and came to be widely read and circulated over a vast region of the early church. This is a level of circulation those other gospels never attained.

Discussion Questions

1. How and when were the books of the New Testament identified as Scripture?
2. What are some of the differences between the books of the New Testament and the books that were excluded?
3. What is some of the evidence used by critics to argue that parts of the New Testament were forged? How might you respond to their arguments?

Contradictions, Contradictions

Why Does My Bible Have All These Mistakes?

At about the time I started to doubt that God had inspired the words of the Bible, I began to be influenced by Bible courses taught from a historical-critical perspective. I started seeing discrepancies in the text. I saw that some of the books of the Bible were at odds with one another. I became convinced by the arguments that some of the books were not written by the authors from whom they were named. And I began to see that many of the traditional Christian doctrines that I long held to be beyond question . . . had moved away from the original teachings of Jesus and his apostles.
—Bart Ehrman[1]

The more I studied the Bible, the less I was prone to accuse the Bible of obvious historical errors and stupid mistakes, including theological errors about a matter as profound as human suffering and evil. To the contrary, I found the Bible rich, complex, varied, and helpful and truthful in dealing with

precisely such life and death matters. . . . In my case, my faith
in the Bible was strengthened, but the opposite seems to have
been the case with Bart.
—BEN WITHERINGTON III[2]

Perhaps you played games as a kid where somebody kept changing the rules as you went along, especially if they were losing or were getting annoyed at not being able to control you. Pretty soon, the foul lines began moving a little closer (when you were batting), the out-of-bounds area was harder to avoid (when you were running), the dolls weren't allowed to pretend what you'd been pretending with them before. The rules eventually became so restrictive, there really wasn't much game left to play anymore. Everybody finally just got mad and threatened to quit.

Take ball. Go home.

It's probably hard to believe, but this same sort of thing (on a much more civil, adult basis, of course) can also occur in the various contests of scholarly debate when one camp insists that certain arbitrary rules *must* be applied to your arguments before they can be considered credible. So the Bible cannot be trusted. And anyone who disagrees is disqualified as a nonexpert.

Now let's be clear: there's nothing wrong with arriving at rules that govern how differing opinions are to be judged and evaluated. Nor is there a problem with coming into a debate carrying one's own assumptions and presuppositions. Each of us has them. But when the result of these "givens" basically shuts down all other views, narrowing the playing field until only one team is legitimately allowed to participate, *then* we have a problem because the opponent's rules claim that no one else really has anything worth saying.

Game over. Before we start.

And that's why—as a preview to this chapter on the Bible's alleged contradictions—we first need to show you how critics will attempt to tilt the playing surface against you, creating a closed, controlled environment in which they alone can win.

It comes down to the distinction between *diversity* and *disagreement*.

Keep those words in mind. They'll appear again.

The Bible, let's remember, is actually a library—a collection of sixty-six books, written across a number of millennia by a wide range of authors differing in background, educational level, occupational lifestyle, and a world of other characteristics. No other book or anthology known to man comes anywhere close—we're talking about "within the same galaxy" close—to representing the stunning scope of the biblical story or the consistency of the biblical message front to back. As familiar as you probably are with the Bible, never let yourself forget how huge it is, both in the length of time it covers and the depth of message it communicates.

And yet when some people detect even a hint of diversity among any of the wide-ranging books of the Bible, they declare it an absolute *contradiction*. Boom. Automatically.

Anywhere the Bible shows *legitimate development* of thought across time—an explanation or interpretation in later Scriptures that couldn't possibly have been contemplated before certain events had happened—they consider it an *irreconcilable difference* with what was said earlier.

Anywhere a particular book supplements or builds on another, as opposed to just repeating the same thing the other has already said, they call it an example of *disagreement* between the two. By their rules that's all there is to it. Case closed. But is it?

Only if you twist the meaning of literary *diversity* and historical *development* until it spells out their definition of undeniable *disagreement* and *contradiction*.

Contradictory Evidence

Ask people why they don't believe the Bible, and many of them will tell you, for one thing, "Because it's just full of contradictions." OK; that's what they've come to believe, so . . . let's go at this another way.

What if we were to hand them a whole bunch of proposed contradictions to choose from? Then we'd all have a chance to see if these claims actually hold up to common sense and careful scrutiny. Surely they wouldn't mind if we just asked some honest questions, would they?

We'll start with two basic questions: *Is every perceived contradiction a real contradiction? Does difference really equal contradiction as some claim?*

Suppose you're sitting around with a bunch of friends, maybe at a restaurant or some other place; and in the flow of conversation, you start telling a story about something you did or saw and the way you remember it. Halfway through, one of your other friends—who was also there and saw the same thing—jumps in and adds an extra detail or two that you'd forgotten or left out. This goes on, back and forth, with maybe other friends occasionally interrupting, laying down a third or fourth perspective onto an experience you each shared in common.

What's happening here?

Since you're not all saying the same words or describing events in exactly the same way, are all but one of you lying? or confused? or being intentionally deceptive? Based on these differences in what you're saying, are you obviously contradicting one another?

Or wouldn't it be much fairer to acknowledge, by contrast, that a person sitting there listening to each of you talk would actually get a much more complete, more interesting, more well-rounded picture of the memory you're all describing?

See why *diversity* doesn't necessarily mean *disagreement*?

The Bible is like that. Instead of the various accounts of Scripture revealing a lack of unity in the overall message, their individual works actually weave a tapestry that's much more compelling and less monochromatic than some one-note, robotic printout or press release. The Bible is not like a government document, processed in triplicate—the pink copy, the blue copy, the goldenrod copy—each punched with the same identical information. No, it's living and breathing. It's layered and textured. It's God's work in real life, in the real world, with real people, living in a real time, not a carefully managed sheet of talking points designed to keep any of its writers from going off message.

Actually, the variety of perspectives found in the Bible—far from being a *threat* to the divine inspiration of Scripture—are part of what proves its validity. If some critics weren't trying so hard to impose a rigid, artificial, OCD structure onto the way God *should* have written his book (if they'd been in charge of things), they might find some highly plausible reasons for why any of these so-called inconsistencies are really among its greatest assets.

For starters we've pulled four test cases from the skeptic's filing cabinet of contradictions, places where they might claim to see disagreement in the Bible's presentation on a number of key details and doctrines: the crucifixion, the virgin birth, the miracles of Jesus, and the relationship of salvation to the Old Testament law.

What you'll see, we believe, is that the statements of these various biblical writers are, yes, *diverse* across time and personalities but not in *disagreement* across the board.

And that means they're not contradictions.

Test Case 1: Differing Accounts of the Crucifixion

The Gospels of Mark and Luke (people like our friend Bart Ehrman object) contain different depictions of the crucifixion. In Mark, Jesus dies in despair, unsure of what's happening to him; in Luke, Jesus seems to be in complete control of the situation.

If you were asked to give an exact, exhaustive depiction of any event you'd personally witnessed that lasted for, say, three hours or more, would you include every tiny detail? Would you leave anything out? At all? If it were a football game, for example, would you report on every single down, every single player, every single product advertised at every single commercial break? If it were a movie or theater production, would you repeat every piece of dialogue, describe the components of every backdrop, catalog every person that appeared in any scene?

No. Even in being very thorough and comprehensive, you'd still be discerning about what you inserted into your retelling of the action.

Likewise, the writers of the Gospels had justifiable reasons for why they mentioned the various details they chose to include and why they left out the ones they chose to omit—part by design, part by necessity. Because as everyone knows, *any historical account is by nature selective.* As John the apostle said, Jesus did so many things during his earthly life, "if they were written one by one, I suppose not even the world itself could contain the books that would be written" (John 21:25).

So as we look at this first case, it appears we should all be able to agree that two authors could decide to highlight *different* aspects of any event. Right? The larger question is: Are these different aspects they portray *incompatible* with one another?

Mark, for his part, recorded only one specific thing Jesus spoke from the cross—"My God, My God, why have You forsaken Me?" (Mark 15:34)—as well as commenting that Jesus later "let out a loud cry" just before he "breathed His last" (v. 37).

Compare this to Luke, who—while not mentioning the one statement Mark recorded—listed three other utterances of Jesus, including what seem to be the actual words of the "loud cry" Mark described at the moment of Jesus' death: "Father, into Your hands I entrust My spirit" (Luke 23:46). In fact, if you read the two accounts side by side, you will see that the citation of this verse appears at the same point as Mark's loud cry. Luke is our friend at the table adding something he knew about the event.

So, yes, in looking at these tight snapshots alone, Luke does seem to emphasize Jesus' resolute awareness and confidence in facing death—"Father, into Your hands I entrust My spirit"— compared to the feeling you get from what Mark describes: "My God, My God, why have You forsaken Me?"

Doubters would call this a *contradiction*. An *incompatibility*.

But wait a minute. Let's not shrink the sample size down to such a narrow portion. Look back at Mark's whole Gospel and see if this incompatibility claim holds up. See if he was intent on describing Jesus as being in the dark about the certainty, the meaning, and the outcome of his death.

Three times in Mark—chapter 8 (vv. 31–38), chapter 9 (vv. 30–35), and chapter 10 (vv. 32–45)—Jesus made predictions concerning his impending death. On one of those occasions, he told his disciples why his death was necessary: "For even the Son of Man did not come to be served, but to serve, and to give His life—a ransom for many" (10:45). He later showed complete awareness in the garden of Gethsemane that Judas, the one who had led the religious leaders out to find him, was his "betrayer" (14:42). And when Jesus appeared before the high priest, he himself delivered the testimony that led directly to his death sentence, declaring himself divine, that they would one day see him "seated at the right hand of the Power and coming with the clouds of heaven" (14:62).

Doesn't sound like someone who was caught off guard by these deadly events!

And what about Luke? Does he only present Jesus as being stoic and determined about his suffering? Does he not also describe him as pleading, imploring in prayer, mere hours before the actual torture began? "Father, if You are willing, take this cup away from Me," Luke records him as saying, while his sweat became "like drops of blood falling to the ground" (Luke 22:42, 44).

So when looking at their entire accounts, this supposedly glaring difference in how Mark and Luke depicted Jesus' suffering sort of blurs and fades away. Sure, it turns out there's some *diversity* in what they said. As we've seen, there's always going to be diversity when different people recount a given story. But not necessarily *disagreement*—especially if these writers were inspired by God, as Scripture claims.

Test Case 2: The Virgin Birth—Now You See It, Now You Don't

The Gospels of Matthew and Luke mention Jesus' virgin birth while Mark and John seem not to be aware of it—or at least don't mention it.

Yes, right off the bat in both Matthew and Luke—first chapters of each book—we hear the stunning, angelic announcement of Jesus' miraculous birth. Joseph learns of it in a dream (Matt. 1:18–25); Mary learns of it face-to-face with an angel (Luke 1:26–38).

But does this mean Mark and John—simply because they didn't include it in their Gospels and chose other ways of describing Jesus' extraordinary life—weren't even *aware* of his virgin birth?

Let's look at Mark first. His Gospel is distinguished from the other three by being characteristically concise. So it's not surprising that, in his rush to start talking about Jesus' ministry, he skips completely over the first thirty years of his life. By verse 9 of the first chapter, Jesus is already up and on the scene as an adult.

Are we to conclude, then, that not only did Mark have no knowledge of Jesus' unusual birth, but he also knew nothing at all that happened to Jesus before he was thirty years old? After all, he doesn't *mention* it, if he does know. As a close associate of both Peter and Paul (Acts 12:12, 25), not to mention as a member of the extremely close-knit early church, how likely would it have been that Mark had never heard—ever—any accounts of this remarkable, supernatural event? Are the things he wrote in his Gospel the *only* things he knew about Jesus?

Come on. That's not only highly implausible historically; it's patently illogical. *Failure to mention something doesn't necessarily equal ignorance.* Nor does it mean denial. It simply means a choice was made not to address something. The fact that Mark starts where he does tells us he made a choice not to discuss Jesus' childhood whatever he may have known about it. Why? Who knows. What one cannot claim is that Mark contradicts Matthew or Luke. Silence does not make a contradiction.

What about the Gospel of John, then? As you may know, his Gospel differs from the other three. Written much later than the others, it tends to focus more on bringing out the deeper theological meaning than on just recording what happened (though, of course, *all* the Gospels are interpreted history, presenting events from a faith perspective). John begins his Gospel account not in traditional reporting style but by declaring that Jesus existed even prior to the creation of the universe. Before time. Before everything. If you think the virgin birth is big, check this out—it's even bigger!

So since John takes this infinitely wider view of Jesus' entrance into the world, perhaps we can forgive him for not being so stiffly specific about the way Jesus' mother got pregnant. Interestingly, his choice is the opposite of Mark's. Where Mark decides to skip the childhood, John decides to start before the birth. Different folks, different strokes, but no contradiction.

Besides, John makes at least a couple of indirect references to the virgin birth as he goes along. He speaks of believers as being people born "not of blood, or of the will of the flesh, or of the will of man, but of God," which is not entirely unlike how "the Word became flesh and took up residence among us" (John 1:13–14). See any hints of the virgin birth there?

Bounce ahead also to John 8—to a lengthy interchange between Jesus and the high-and-mighty Pharisees, who peppered him with acrobatic questions designed to trip him up. One of their sharper digs came in verse 41, where they arrogantly tried to elevate themselves above Jesus' pedigree: "*We* weren't born of sexual immorality. . . . *We* have one Father—God." (The likely implication: "But we're not so sure about *you*.")

Oooh. Hear the derision. Questioning his ancestry. They apparently were in on the snide, juicy, gossipy rumor about Jesus' mysterious birth story. No father. Unwed mother. Later writings, in fact, repeat this very charge, denying the paternity of God the Father in Jesus' birth.[3]

So here's the question, based on the lack of specificity in Mark and John about the virgin birth: If God didn't see fit to inform half of the eventual Gospel writers about this vital occurrence—the Holy Spirit miraculously placing the life of God's Son into the womb of a mortal village girl—then how can their writings be considered inspired?

And here's our comeback question: Isn't it just as likely (*much more likely*, in fact) they were all aware of this widely known story but simply chose to describe the incomparable Jesus in other ways equally amazing?

Does leaving something out in deference to something else mean they were indisputably in disagreement over a key piece of doctrine? Isn't the point of having four Gospels the diversity of having four different perspectives?

Test Case 3: Are They Miracles, or Are They Signs?

In Matthew, Jesus refuses to perform a miracle to prove his deity. But in John, Jesus' spectacular deeds are *intentionally designed* to convince people of his true identity. In fact, John specifically calls them "signs" as opposed to just "miracles."

To try pitting John's testimony against that of the other Gospel writers—as if his views on miracles were in direct contradiction with theirs—is to see all trees and no forest. It ignores the reasons behind John's writing.

John, as we've said, wrote his volume at a later date than the others. And so he almost assuredly built on the literature (or at least, the tradition) that was previously existent. One of us (Andreas) has identified at least twenty such instances where

John took a motif found in Matthew, Mark, and Luke and developed it further theologically.[4]

John's use of the word "sign" is one of those occurrences. Where the other Gospels regularly referred to Jesus' healings, his exorcisms, and his mastery over nature as "miracles," John apparently sought to make the *theological* point that what was most significant about these powerhouse displays was not their wow factor but rather their ability to induce faith in Christ. Of what lasting good were Jesus' miracles if all they did was to transfix, not transform?

They were signposts, pointing people to God.

But it's not as though this idea was foreign to the earlier Gospel writers. Even in Matthew, where Jesus twice refused to perform a miracle on demand (12:38–39; 16:1–4), he still made clear that the intended effect of his wonders was to produce a heart change, to inspire true belief. So when Jesus said, for example, "If the miracles that had been done in you had been done in Tyre and Sidon, they would have repented in sackcloth and ashes" (Matt. 11:21), he was saying that inducing repentance was exactly what his miracles were supposed to do. Luke noted the eternal intention behind Jesus' supernatural acts as well when he quoted Jesus as saying, "If I drive out demons by the finger of God, then the kingdom of God has come to you" (Luke 11:20).

So these *miracles* were actually *signs* all along—even in Matthew, Mark, and Luke—by nature if not by name.[5] And yet his miracles were not so mechanical and one-dimensional that Jesus didn't realize some people would only want to see them for sport and spectacle.

Therefore, even in John—where some people detect such a vast contradiction between "signs" and "miracles"—Jesus was careful to show that while any kind of belief is better than unbelief, something is always inferior about a faith that relies mainly on miracles. His initial reply to one particular man's plea, for example, was to chide him, to challenge him: "Unless you people see signs and wonders, you will not believe" (John 4:48). Most famously of all, in response to the believing words of "doubting Thomas" after seeing the resurrected Christ with his own eyes, Jesus said, "Because you have seen Me, you have believed," but "those who believe without seeing" are the ones who are truly blessed (John 20:29).

John was not changing the tenor of Jesus' miracles as presented in the other Gospels but was simply employing a more descriptive term—"signs"—to further illumine the theological depths already dug by those who had gone before. To put it in musical terms, John wasn't creating a whole new melody; he was merely *transposing* the melody that had already been sounded in the other Gospels, setting it into a slightly different key.[6]

Again, we see *diversity* but not *contradiction*.

Test Case 4: Saved by Works or Saved by Grace?

Matthew and Paul (some claim) are in contradiction on salvation and the law.

OK, here's the last one we'll look at in this section. And it's a little trickier. Bonus points if you hang in there through this one. Otherwise, if you've seen enough evidence already, just skip to the next section ("Putting It Together").

"Don't assume that I came to destroy the Law," Jesus said near the beginning of his Sermon on the Mount (Matt. 5:17). "The Law" represented the vast sea of Old Testament Scripture—familiarly known as "the Law and the Prophets"—the only Scripture known to that generation. Jesus was declaring that this ancient testimony, which had guided God's people through the long centuries of their existence, was not to be wadded up and thrown away just because the promised Messiah was now on the scene (momentous occasion though it was).

But was Matthew actually trying to make Jesus say a lot more than that? When he recorded Jesus saying, "Unless your righteousness surpasses that of the scribes and Pharisees, you will never enter the kingdom of heaven" (Matt. 5:20), was his point that strict observance of the Mosaic law was now more crucially important than ever?

Bart Ehrman thinks so. And he cannot fathom how the God who purportedly put words like those into the pen of Matthew is the same God who had instructed Paul to write words like these: "Now, *apart from the law*, God's righteousness has been revealed" (Rom. 3:21).

Ehrman says, "If Matthew, who wrote some twenty-five or thirty years after Paul, ever read any of Paul's letters, he certainly did not find them inspiring, let alone inspired," since "Matthew thinks that they as followers of Jesus need to keep the law. In fact, they need to keep it even better than most religious Jews."[7] Paul, on the other hand (Ehrman continues), says that "getting into the kingdom . . . is made possible only by the death and resurrection of Jesus." That's it. No law-abiding necessary.

In fact, "for gentiles, keeping the Jewish law (for example, circumcision) is strictly forbidden."[8]

So . . . maybe he's got a point there.

It really does sound like a difference, doesn't it?

But as usual, being hot on the scent of a contradiction can often blind a person to the rest of their surroundings, causing them to ignore some available clues that might lead to a far different conclusion. There is more to this story than initially meets the eye.

First, *they're reading only half of what Jesus said*. The main point of what he was saying in Matthew 5:17 has less to do with his "not destroying" or "not abolishing" the Old Testament law and more to do with his role in "fulfilling" it—a point Matthew drove home time and again in his Gospel (Matt. 1:22; 2:15, 17, 23; 4:14; 8:17; 12:17; 13:35; 21:4; 27:9). Jesus, he maintained, is the completion of the law, the total expression of the law, the full-bodied fulfillment of perfection the Old Testament had been pointing toward all along. So Matthew 5:19—"Whoever practices and teaches these commands will be called great in the kingdom of heaven"—refers not backward to a technical observance of the law but forward toward the true heart obedience we now can actually live out . . . because of Christ, who has fulfilled the law.

Jesus is pushing here not for fulfilling the letter of the law, but seeing where the law leads: to an integrity of life extending from the heart into action. So it's not just murder but anger, not just adultery but lust, not just divorce but keeping your vows. Doing this fulfills the law. Seen in this light, this is like Paul, who calls us to love, truth, and imitation of the Lord (1 Cor. 10:31–11:1; Phil. 4:8–9).

Second, *they're overlooking Matthew's appeal to grace.* If Matthew was so intent on saying that adherence to the law was more paramount than ever, then he likely wouldn't have started off his transcription of Jesus' Sermon on the Mount with the words, "Blessed are the poor in spirit" (Matt. 5:3 KJV). Right from the start, he allows Jesus to be remembered for urging people to recognize and admit their desperate spiritual condition before God.

That's not exactly a statement of do-goodism.

Then, as Jesus continues throughout Matthew 5 to expose the depths of human frailty—by forbidding not only murder but even the *anger* that leads to murder (vv. 21–22), by forbidding not only adultery but even the *lust* that leads to adultery (vv. 27–28)—he anticipates the words of Paul: "There is no one righteous, not even one. . . . For all have sinned and fall short of the glory of God" (Rom. 3:10, 23). As one writer has said, "What Paul is explaining in Romans and Galatians, Jesus is doing in the Sermon on the Mount."[9] In whichever place you read, you see humankind in need of God's help and favor, not earning our way by good deeds into his good graces. What good work we do is a product of grace, not its cause (Eph. 2:8–10).

Third, *they're missing Christ's focus on motive and attitude when it comes to obeying the law.* Matthew notes where Jesus does things that challenge the law. He does it even within Matthew 5 when he cites Exodus 21:24 in verse 38. Here he reprioritizes what the law taught. The chapter as a whole is showing Jesus is not reading the law as merely rules to be fulfilled, but he is stressing that the heart attitude the law calls for be followed as well. He is pushing his audience for a faithful character before God, which is exactly what Paul teaches in Galatians 5:18–23. As far as Christ is concerned, men corrupted the law by their immoral attitude toward God.

So let's wrap this test case up this way. There is more similarity between the Gospels and Paul's letters than some people would tell you. We hope you can see that. And yet there are obviously some differences too.

But do you know who'd have the most problem explaining themselves if everything you read in Paul were *exactly* the same as what you read in the Gospels?

We would, that's who.

Think about it. Jesus was preaching to people (in Matthew) *before* they'd witnessed his death and resurrection. Even his own disciples, despite being told on a regular basis that he was going to be killed and would rise again—didn't get it. And they were the ones closest to him.

So imagine what your religion professor would say if the Gospel writers had put into Jesus' mouth a fully developed theology for the key events in his life—his death, burial, and resurrection—events that hadn't happened yet, events that hadn't become a part of world history and anyone else's experience. Would that have sounded like an authentic conversation? It would have been like talking in past tense about a dress some actress wore to next year's Oscars. The fact that the Gospel writers, each composing their work many years after Jesus' life on earth, did not doctor his words to make them sound more like Paul's doesn't force the two into contradiction. If anything, it's another proof that their writings are historically accurate. It's a testament to their integrity and honesty. They were *recording* history (and responsibly interpreting it), not *rewriting* it by altering the facts or changing the message.

But then when Paul came along after Jesus' death, resurrection, and ascension, he was splashing down into another pool of history entirely. The cross and empty tomb were by that time permanent fixtures of the past, ready to be dealt with and described through Jesus' followers subsequent to his death. That's why we see an *understandable progression* of thought and theology flowing from what Jesus had said on earth to what Paul and others said about him afterward.

There's value—even virtue—in the *diversity*.

And nowhere does it spell actual *disagreement*.

Putting It Together

Perhaps you've been reeled in before by the gavel-to-gavel television coverage of a high profile courtroom case. The prosecution lays out their version of what happened; then the defense counters with their own testimony and witnesses. And by the time the jury is sent back to chambers to arrive at a verdict, their job is to what?—to see if they can gather up all the information they've heard and piece it back together into a smooth, single, comprehensive flow of events.

They're *harmonizing* the material.

That's because no one individual who took the witness stand told every detail, start to finish, of the whole series of circumstances involved in the case. But in the end, by laying everything on top of everything else, the jury works with all the stray bits of evidence to craft a reasonable time line and to recreate in their mind the big picture.

Historians do this all the time. When dealing with ancient history, they're basically *forced* to. They'll read dozens, perhaps hundreds of books, articles, and samples of written correspondence; they'll listen to tapes and lectures and personal interviews; they'll research as many accounts as they can find on whatever subject they're seeking to capture: a war, a time period, a movement, a presidency. Then finally, ultimately, they're able to present a pieced-together summary of what they believe happened, in what order, all in relation to what other things were going on at the same time.

It's a harmony. A composite. A fusion.

Now some people don't think the Bible—if it had been written the way it was supposed to—should require harmonization. If it's inspired by God, the details should be abundantly clear, without any question or suspicion to be sorted out. If they had been in charge of writing the Bible, they sure would've done a better job of keeping it perfectly consistent in every place. Seems like that's something God should be able to do.

Yes, that makes for a good stump speech. It's designed to rattle your cage and make you feel like you've caught God in an awkward, weakened position. But this whole line of thought is curious, considering that harmonization is so standard a practice among historians and considering how long ago the events of Scripture took place. Apparently what's acceptable for studying Alexander the Great or Julius Caesar or Mozart or Babe Ruth just doesn't get to apply to Jesus and the Bible. Just because.

So rather than being free to create a full look at Jesus' trial, for example, by meshing Mark's account (which was short and to the point) with John's account (which includes a lot more dialogue and detail), we're just told these guys were mixed up, out of sync, that their Gospels can't be harmonized.

But why not? What rule says we're allowed only one book—"Jesus: The Authorized Biography"—and that's all? Why is this the only way God could have done it and still declare his Word inspired? The early church painted a much more harmonious picture. They looked at the four Gospels in our Bible as actually *one* Gospel, written "according to" four different witnesses—Matthew, Mark, Luke, and John: "the fourfold Gospel"![10] They *wanted* the diversity. They *liked* the various perspectives. It painted a richer, fuller picture of who Jesus is.

The same goes for evaluating so-called "contradictions" in Scripture that deal with *time lines*—descriptions of what happened when, what happened first, what happened next. Why doesn't it always sound the same? Why aren't events always presented in the same order?

Ancient literature from the period of the Gospels was consistently less worried about putting things in chronological order than arranging them by theme and topic. That's just a fact. So, for example, when Luke reported the tearing of the temple veil *before* Jesus' death (Luke 23:44–46) and Matthew and Mark mentioned it *after* Jesus' death (Matt. 27:50; Mark 15:37–39), there's a pretty simple reason for the rearrangement.

According to ceremonial law, the heavily embroidered curtain they were referencing separated the holy of holies from the rest of the inner temple (2 Chron. 3:14), signifying a place that was accessible only to the high priest, and then only once a year on the Day of Atonement (Heb. 6:7). So this rending of the temple veil that coincided with Jesus' crucifixion—"split in two from top to bottom" (Matt. 27:51)—was keenly symbolic of what his death meant: the removal of all barriers between man and God. It was an epic, illustrative miracle.

Matthew and Luke, being much more descriptive than Mark, chose to group this amazing wonder alongside some of the other cosmic signs that occurred on that momentous day—the midnight darkness at noontime, the rumble of a rock-splitting earthquake, resurrected bodies emerging from their opened tombs—presenting these events in no particular order. The added weight of sorting them out chronologically resonates more with the mind-set of our *modern* thinking. That's the way we typically process events today when we retell and research them. But we're being a bit arrogant and unforgiving to force our linear perspectives onto writers of earlier times who just weren't as accustomed to orienting their histories in that fashion. Only by equating *good* scholarship with *skeptical* scholarship can a person feign surprise at the chronological flexibilities that commonly exist within ancient texts.

These writers weren't lying, either in this case or in others, where the time line of Jesus' life appears slightly askew. They and their original readers and hearers just weren't always hung up on the same things that preoccupy us today.

It's *diversity*, not *disagreement*. One simply chose to present the detail as part of another theme they saw as more relevant than giving chronology. And as writers they have the right to make those choices.

Yes, harmonization can be a somewhat messy process in spots. We admit that. Just like in a courtroom, a few loose ends can pop up where the pieces don't exactly fit together. But in case after case in Scripture, as seen in the examples we studied earlier in the chapter, solid arguments can be made for why they appear the way they do.

"A" Big Problem

The granddaddy of all contradictions in Bart Ehrman's mind—the one at which he said "the floodgates opened" for him when he recognized it[11]—concerns what's actually a minor citation yet is admittedly a bit confusing. Interesting to investigate. But in Ehrman's judgment he deemed it sufficient grounds for making a gigantic leap away from his former belief in the divine inspiration of the Bible.[12]

This was the straw, and his faith was the camel's back.

Just to be sure we're communicating: the Gospels (you probably know) are not entirely different from one another. Especially in Matthew, Mark, and Luke—which are known as the Synoptic Gospels (a composite of two Greek words meaning "viewed together")—many of the same stories from Jesus' life might appear in two of them, sometimes in all three of them. In certain cases the different renderings are almost word for word the same; in other instances they may differ slightly; in yet other cases the difference may be more substantial.

Matthew 12:1–8; Mark 2:23–28; and Luke 6:1–5 include a story where Jesus and his disciples were walking through a grain field on the Sabbath day, picking off heads of grain as they went.

They were hungry. But it was the Sabbath. So when spotted by some nitpicking Pharisees, Jesus and his men found themselves accused of some serious naughtiness: law breaking.

Jesus responded to this charge by recalling a thousand-year-old scene from King David's early life (1 Sam. 21:1–6) when David and his young band of warriors had stopped off hungry at the high priest's door but found that the only available bread in the house was the sacred loaves that had been dedicated for the worship of God. The priest, however, decided to give them the consecrated bread anyway.

This priest's name, according to 1 Samuel 21, was Ahimelech. But that's not what Mark said.

Mark is the only one of the Gospel writers who, when recounting this event (Mark 2:26), chose to identify the Old Testament story to which Jesus had referred by saying it happened when there was a high priest on duty named . . . Abiathar.

So which is it, everybody? Ahimelech or Abiathar?

Problem.

Again, this was the touchstone that sent Bart Ehrman over the edge of Christian belief. If the God who supposedly created and maintains the atmospheric chemistry of planet Earth cannot keep one of his Gospel writers from going to the stack of names under "High Priests Starting with Letter A" and picking the wrong card from the deck, how can he still expect us to believe he is so all wise and powerful?

You're wanting a contradiction? You're wanting to know why these independent Gospels can't just be harmonized and their discrepancies glossed over? "Try *this* one!" Ehrman says.

Ahimelech. Abiathar. There's no harmony for that!

OK, it's certainly possible that these two names got confused—if not originally, then at some point along the way. Anybody can see that. It's reasonable.

But is this the only possibility? Can you not think of any others at all?

Here, we'll try two.

The little Greek word *epi* used in Mark 2:26 right before the words "Abiathar the high priest" is normally translated *upon*. But in this case *upon* would make little sense. You wouldn't say that some event happened "*upon* Abiathar the high priest." Yet as anyone who's tried learning another language will tell you, words have a range of meanings. The tricky part is learning which meaning should be used when. What then could *epi* be saying here, if not *upon*? There are two prime candidates.

Option 1—Time

It could indicate the *time* at which the event occurred. Like the way we might refer to the Eisenhower years. Or the Michael Jordan era. It's not always a technically defined period of time but more of a general season in history. And Abiathar, who was the much more recognizable high-priestly name from that age, having been the only survivor of King Saul's maniacal slaughter of priests in 1 Samuel 22, would have been the quickest connection point for Mark's first-century audience. More so than Ahimelech.

Something similar appears to happen in Luke 3:2, where Annas and Caiaphas are both said to be high priests during Jesus' ministry, even though both men were never officially high priest at the same time. Still, no one can legitimately accuse

Luke of making an error, since while Caiaphas was actually
the high priest, his father-in-law Annas remained a significant
figure who could still be called "the high priest." It's sort of how
we still refer to U.S. presidents as "President Bush" or "President
Clinton," even when they're no longer in office or, looking back,
not yet in office. Why couldn't Mark have been doing that?

Option 2—Location

It could also be indicating the place where the original
story was *located* in Old Testament Scripture. The Bible hadn't
yet been divided into chapters and verses when Mark was writing. So when referring to stories that came from the existing
Hebrew Scriptures, he could only get his readers into the
ballpark. He did the same thing another time in Mark 12:26,
where he quoted Jesus as saying, "Haven't you read in the book
of Moses, in the passage about the burning bush . . ." He didn't
say, ". . . in Exodus 3." He just meant to tell people that he was
referring to that general area in the scrolls where it talks about
God first appearing to Moses. And in the case of Abiathar,
whose first appearance in Scripture falls directly after the story
that's recounted in the Gospel, Mark's rationale may have been
to help his reader more clearly bookmark the location he was
talking about.

Can we be sure about that? No. But these are at least reasonable hypotheses.

If the confusion in wording over Ahimelech and Abiathar is
truly where Ehrman gave up on the Bible, we humbly wish he
was still open to considering some other plausibilities. Because
as with every other contradiction the Bible is accused of, these

things are simply not as open-and-shut as the skeptics would suggest.

Why can't we hear the Bible sing with just a little harmony?

Repeat Business

Some people who champion the freedom of diversity will not tolerate the presence of diversity in the Bible. Some people who accuse Christianity of being so off-key will not allow the Bible to harmonize its way into cohesion. And some people who think we're ridiculously foolish to hold onto our faith are perhaps too slow to allow us the common courtesy of using our common sense.

Here's a little analogy to help you see what we mean.

Just for a moment let's assume you're enough of a groupie for a certain band or musical performer, you might be tempted one year (if you had the time and money) to take in as many as three or four of their concerts on whatever tour they were doing. You saw them in Nashville, in Atlanta, in Orlando, and even once in California, a lot farther away from home. No doubt you detected a good bit of scripting in the various performances you saw. The song order was a lot the same. Some of the same jokes and one-liners appeared at the same part of the show. But because you became so familiar with the general flow of the evening, you particularly noticed when they would personalize their banter for the local crowd—"Hello, Chicago! How 'bout them Cubs?"—or when they reconfigured their set of material slightly from one of the previous concerts you'd seen. You would actually have been disappointed, to tell you the truth, if being there in person had been like listening to the exact same "live" recording every single time.

The harshest skeptics are often guilty of treating the biblical account of Jesus' life as if it's a series of "one night only" events and that whatever he might have said, done, or taught in one town or one setting comprised the *only time* he ever said, did, or taught those particular things. And so if we ever hear one of the Gospels use a different word from another Gospel in recalling something Jesus said, then the Bible is obviously misquoting him (which wouldn't help the "divine inspiration" argument very much, would it?).

But why should we assume this? Why is it odd to think that Jesus wouldn't have spoken on certain topics more than once? In different venues? (Remember: like the traveling band above, Jesus was a traveling preacher.) It's not as if people who didn't hear Jesus in person that day could check his Twitter feed or catch the report later on CNN. Would his every appearance in every town include nothing but all-new material? And did he possess so little personality or awareness of each audience that he never varied his delivery from place to place?

Like any good teacher, wouldn't he have taught often by repetition, reinforcing his intended principles, giving them more opportunities to stick in his listeners' heads and hearts? Might he react to a real-time event by stating a previously spoken truth but cast it in a way that matched the situation?

Of course. Logic.

One common "contradiction" of this kind involves Jesus' statements in Matthew 12:30—"Anyone who is not with Me is against Me"—and Mark 9:40—"Whoever is not against us is for us." Read those two again, and you'll quickly see the few switch-arounds in wording.

But don't just read the words. Check the context.

In Matthew, Jesus was aiming his comments at a group of Pharisees who were saying under their breath that his power to cast out demons came from the devil himself. In Mark, how-ever, Jesus was talking to his own disciples (the "us" in his state-ment), who were complaining about how they'd seen another follower of Christ, one who didn't belong to their tight little group, casting out demons in Jesus' name. Didn't he know that was *their* job? So they had tried to stop him. Obviously, then, these statements of Jesus recorded in Matthew and Mark were not spoken at the same time, to the same audience, or with the same intention, even though they do communicate a similar message.

Then Luke, barging his way into the proceedings, gives the most ringing support to our argument of all. Proving that *he* saw no contradiction or double vision in what had happened, he actually included *both* of these stories in his account (Luke 9:50; 11:23)! So if these statements are somehow in conflict, then Luke was apparently conflicted within himself.

Another noted "contradiction" in Scripture—the Roman centurion who issued a statement of belief at the moment of Jesus' death—has less to do with *context* and more to do with the purpose of writing.

The Gospel writers, remember, were not submitting their manuscripts to a publishing house, hoping their works might one day be printed in your Bible. We believe, of course, that God's Spirit led them to write. But even if someone wants to take this inspirational motivation out of the picture, these men still had their own personal reasons for penning their histories.

- *Matthew*, for instance, wrote from a Jewish standpoint, seeking to show that Jesus was the long-prophesied Messiah.
- *Mark* was describing Jesus Christ throughout his Gospel as the authoritative, powerful Son of God.
- *Luke* is the first of a two-part history together with the book of Acts, addressed more specifically to a Greek audience, making a case among unbelievers for Jesus' authority and authenticity.
- *John* emphasized Jesus' deity and the need to believe in him, to know him, to receive eternal life.

So Mark, in mentioning the centurion, quotes him as saying of Jesus, "This man really was *God's Son!*" (Mark 15:39). Mark is telling us climatically who the Christ is. When Luke recorded this same scene, he quoted him as saying, "This man really was *righteous!*" (Luke 23:47).

Contradiction?

As one commentator has noted, "One's 'righteous' status is surely implied in the title 'son of God,' making these terms fairly interchangeable. . . . [And] given Mark's preference for the 'son of God' theme, and given Luke's concern to prove to the authorities that Jesus (and Christians) were innocent, these differences are quite intelligible."[13]

So do the Gospels occasionally differ in details? Yes.

But again, does this handcuff the Bible to contradictions? Not at all.

The Myth of the Evolving Jesus

One last, main point concerning contradictions, and this is an important one because it deals with some issues surrounding a skepticism you'll hear all the time in religion class as well as in the general culture: Jesus may have been a real man and a great teacher, but that doesn't mean he's God.

What some of the more liberal-leaning Bible scholars have concluded is that the "divinity of Christ" doctrine was not original with Jesus but was rather tacked on later in response to pressure from Greek culture, whose pantheon (Zeus, Poseidon, Athena, and so forth) was central to their worship. If Christians expected to make a dent in the first-century clash of ideas, they needed not just a Christ ("the anointed one") but a *God*.

That's why those who became known as followers of Jesus, the skeptics contend, eventually felt the need to say things like . . .

> Even if there are so-called gods, whether in
> heaven or on earth—as there are many "gods"
> and many "lords"—yet for us there is one God,
> the Father. All things are from Him, and we
> exist for Him. And there is one Lord, Jesus
> Christ. All things are through Him, and we
> exist through Him. (1 Cor. 8:5–6)

> He is the image of the invisible God, the
> firstborn over all creation. For everything was
> created by Him, in heaven and on earth, the
> visible and the invisible, whether thrones or
> dominions or rulers or authorities—all things

> have been created through Him and for Him.
> He is before all things, and by Him all things
> hold together. (Col. 1:15–17)

> So that at the name of Jesus every knee will
> bow—of those who are in heaven and on earth
> and under the earth—and every tongue should
> confess that Jesus Christ is Lord, to the glory
> of God the Father. (Phil. 2:10–11)

And while anyone today can decide for themselves whether or not they believe Jesus is the Son of God, it's hard to follow the skeptical argument presented here: that the whole idea of assigning divinity onto the person of Jesus came along post-Gospel. Because do you know when these quoted verses from 1 Corinthians, Colossians, and Philippians were written?

Before the Gospels.

This means at least by the mid-fifties and early sixties AD (in fact, most likely much earlier), Christians were already regarding Christ as the preexistent, divine Son of God. "The inclusion of Jesus in the unique divine identity," writes Richard Bauckham, "was central to the faith of the early church even before any of the New Testament writings were written." Although we can track development of this thought through the Scriptures and over time, "the decisive step of so including him," he says, "was made at the beginning."[14]

And actually you can see it starting a long time before that.

British scholar N. T. Wright has ably delved into the Old Testament, surveying passages from Exodus, Leviticus, 1 Samuel, 1 Kings, and Isaiah, as well as other writings of the period, helping us see how first-century Jews understood God and his actions in the world.[15] His study has shown "ample evidence that most second-Temple Jews who gave any thought to the matter were hoping for YHWH to return, to dwell once again in the Temple in Jerusalem as he had done in the time of the old monarchy."[16]

(YHWH, by the way, equals the word *Yahweh*, the name of God in Hebrew.)

Wright says first-century Jews talked about God and his activity in several specific ways: Temple, Torah, Wisdom, Logos, and Spirit. So "when we come to the Gospels with those given ways of speaking in our heads," he says, "we discover Jesus behaving—not just talking, but behaving—as if somehow those five ways are coming true in a new manner in what he is doing."[17] Jesus presents himself as the temple, for example (Mark 14:58, among others). He declares his fulfillment of Old Testament law speaking "like one who had authority" (Matt. 7:29), teaching as the Word, living by the Spirit. "So what we see is not so much Jesus going around saying, 'I am the Second Person of the Trinity. Either believe it or not.' That really isn't the way to read the Gospels. Rather, reading them as first-century historians, we can see that Jesus is behaving in ways that altogether say: this whole great story about God who comes to be with his people is actually happening."[18]

And in case his own disciples didn't get it—which they mostly didn't during his lifetime (see Mark 6:52; 7:18; 8:33)—you can bet the religious establishment did, even though they rejected him in unbelief. When Jesus said in Mark 14:62 (as well as Matt. 26:64 and Luke 22:69) that they would see him sitting with God in heaven, they knew he was claiming divinity.[19] They didn't need to wait twenty or thirty years for the Christians to start campaigning for it.

Or think of Paul processing Jesus' appearance to him as described in Acts 9. He knows immediately who the Lord is and how he was seen. This is the faith he writes about in the fifties and sixties when he presents Jesus as God, as we just saw. But he experienced this reality he writes about in the thirties!

All of this doesn't deny, of course, that John's Gospel (written later) is much more explicit than the others in contemplating the divinity of Christ, just as Ehrman and others claim. But still, the Synoptic Gospels do present "in seed form" what would flower into a fuller understanding of the incarnation: "The seed is there, the entire genetic coding for the growth that later takes place."[20] And Paul's experience and writing fit with this hand in glove.

Jesus is God all along in Scripture.

No contradiction.

Contradictions under Control

We're wrapping things up now.

When approaching the Bible, its history, and really any other field of study, always try to avoid two extremes: *credulity* (the readiness to believe anything on slight or no evidence) and its darker twin, *skepticism*. In someone like Bart Ehrman's case, he seems to have exchanged one for the other. And now any question mark is for him an exclamation point.

A *contradiction*.

But let's just state for the record that the Scripture—particularly the New Testament—really orbits around three central themes: (1) there is one God; (2) Jesus is the Messiah and exalted Lord; and (3) the Christian community has been entrusted with the proclamation of the gospel.[21] Other common themes exist, of course, but these three consistently appear as the main pillars of the biblical narrative. So as one author has said, "The question we must ask is not whether these books all say the same thing but whether they all bear witness to the same Jesus."[22] And by any objective standard, they remarkably do.

The early church, for its part, viewed the diversity of the New Testament documents as an *advantage* rather than a *liability*. They didn't conspire to get rid of the four Gospels and enshrine one official version as the exclusive witness to the events surrounding Jesus' life. They understood that four distinct, historical sources proved much more helpful in giving a richer portrait of Christ than any one source ever could, no matter how detailed.

Does this decision on God's part leave us with questions like the ones we've presented in this chapter? Yes, it does—though, again, the answers to these questions are simply not as cut-and-dried as some people would like you to believe.

Can we prove with absolute certainty that our positions are right? No, not always. But neither can anyone else prove they're wrong. We're not belittling others for holding their positions, but why must our reasoned conclusions be declared absurd and out of bounds—against the rules—even if people want to toss out the spiritual belief that resides within them?

In many ways this tension we feel tells us a lot about God and his purposes, his willingness to bring his perfection into human history. Some critics seem to be saying that if God insists on his Book being held up as unique in the history of literature, then the Bible is susceptible to its own unique forms of scrutiny. And my, has it ever been! No other writing has withstood and survived so many investigations into its authenticity—which is all well and good. Bring it on! But how truly amazing and indicative of God, rather than creating some mystical Word that exists in some unknown, unworldly realm of communication all by itself, he chose instead to use normal men, writing in normal ways, operating within the normal rules and customs of their day.

How much more authentic is *that*?

Many of us know that our own personal encounter with the gospel—the forgiveness of sin, the walk of purity, and the promise of heaven—often feels like a rocky, unsteady, occasionally unpleasant experience. It started with our need for Christ's shed blood, and now—even after being captured by his love—our inborn resistance continues to create friction as we live out the gospel's upside-down implications. But just because we don't always know what's good for us doesn't mean we can't be made to see the truth by faith. And God is infinitely patient and persistent with us as we jerkily attempt to learn of him and conform ourselves to his nature and character.

Similarly, both the scholar and the student's encounter with Scripture at times can feel discordant, unwieldy, hard to manage and understand. And yet by inviting truth into our exploration, we can find much peace in our struggle, both with ourselves and with others—not by believing just because we believe it but believing because it is entirely reasonable to do so.

That's how something like *legitimate diversity* can hold its own against the claims of *skeptical disagreement*. And when allowed to compete on the basis of fair ground rules, contradictions begin falling by the wayside one by one.

Discussion Questions

1. What is the difference between legitimate diversity and contradiction?
2. Have you ever had a particular experience with a friend in which you recounted the story in different ways? Was it a matter of one of you getting the facts wrong, or did you just tell the story in different ways?
3. How might Jesus' itinerant ministry (he traveled around preaching to different groups) have led to some of the differences we see in the Gospels?

5

I'll Need an Original

How Can Copies of Copies Be the Same as the Real Thing?

One of the things that people misunderstand, of course—especially my nineteen-year-old students from North Carolina—is that when we're reading the Bible, we're not actually reading the words of Matthew, Mark, Luke, John, or Paul. We're reading translations of the originals of Matthew, Mark, Luke, John, or Paul, because we don't have the originals of any of the books of the New Testament. What we have are copies made centuries later—in most instances, many centuries later.
—BART EHRMAN[1]

Ehrman's book [Misquoting Jesus], *though intending to weaken certainty about the New Testament text, actually demonstrates how the abundance of manuscripts and the antiquity of manuscripts, when run through the mill of textual-critical methodology, allow us to know with a high level of probability what the evangelists and other New Testament authors wrote.*
—MARK ROBERTS[2]

The Bible. How'd it get here?

Not the makeup of the canon. That was chapter 3. But the words on the page, the sentence structure, the way it reads. How did all of *that* stuff transverse the centuries from then till now?

The Bible certainly didn't fall magically from heaven, written in English, typed in twelve-point Times New Roman, complete with colorful maps, bound with a leather cover (or with some polyurethane blend designed to *look* like leather)! But most people who carry their Bibles around today probably haven't given much thought to it.

Have you?

What did the Bible look like at first? How was it duplicated and produced, especially in earliest times? Were there quality controls in place to keep it consistent and accurate across the years? Is there a chance that what we call our Bible today contains errors? Typos? Are we sure it's entirely based on what was written by the original authors? How do we know? How *can* we know?

While such questions are enough to make some people doubt the Bible's authenticity as Bart Ehrman contends, we ourselves have asked the same questions and have each come out on the other side with even stronger trust in the Bible.

So that's what this chapter is all about. No, you won't hear us dodging how we, like scholars of all stripes, might wish that the laborious copying process which preserved the text of Scripture could have been more foolproof than it was. But as you'll see, the fact that God didn't run the whole operation out of a quick-print shop at the corner of First and Golden Street hardly wipes the Bible clean of his fingerprints.

So let's start by using what we know.

Whenever you make a copy of something now, you scan it, or you print it out, or you lay it on the glass of a copy machine, and it comes out exactly the way you put it in. Word for word, just like the original. But long before modern office equipment, and even many centuries before Gutenberg's invention of the printing press in the 1400s, the Bible was already making its journey forward in time, being written out painstakingly by hand.

Which, we admit, was not exactly Xerox.

Think of it—if you were to try copying by hand just the few thousand words from a single chapter of this book, even with good lighting and a brand new ink pen, you'd find out pretty quickly the enormous amount of concentration and skill required to complete the job, to make it look nice, and most importantly to keep from making mistakes, even minor ones. You might look up, for instance, and realize you'd skipped a whole line when you stopped to rub your eyes. You duplicated a word. Probably misspelled a few. Got tired and sloppy. Lost your train of thought. Any of these things could happen. And what if, like the scribes of ancient history, you weren't copying down what you saw in front of you but rather what was being read to you aloud? That'd make the job even tougher, wouldn't it? Sometimes they were copied as a person read aloud what the text said and multiple listeners each made a copy. These copies were compared to look for mistakes that might have been made. By comparing several copies that were written at the same time, most mistakes were caught. But it was possible that mistakes were made and not discovered immediately.

So it's true that among the many handwritten copies of Bible text made throughout history (technically known as *manuscripts*), the possibility of human error was always present. After all, the transmission of the Bible, just like that of other books, was entrusted to the common duplicating methods of the age. Mistakes could be made. They were never more than a pen stroke away. And so if you compared today some of those ancient and medieval manuscripts against one another, side by side, you'd find in certain places a few differences between this copy and that copy. And you wouldn't like it.

If you are not in the habit of comparing ancient manuscripts in your free time to notice differences and mistakes, don't worry. For centuries different groups of people have been studying these things. They know and have cataloged for us where the differences are. Some have sought to make sense of it all. Others have seen only problems. All are asking fair questions. But the discussion is an old one. In fact, a discipline called Textual Criticism is named for it. It does not engage in "criticism" of the text but a careful analysis of what the text was and is.

So this study makes for a fascinating story. For some, it represents a challenge regarding what the Bible is—and whether we can trust it as Ehrman questions. But the Bible has so many copies that we can be confident about the wording of the copies, at least down to what the real options are (as the margins in your translation sometimes also show with a marginal note that says "or" and then gives another rendering).

Once you've seen how the copying and what we know about it works, then you'll see that we can trust the copies we have in our hands and that claims that we cannot are exaggerations about the nature of our texts.

Some critics may believe there are reasons to doubt what we have, but there's really not that much to those claims.

By the Numbers

Let's start by spreading out the whole catalog of biblical manuscripts so you can see the grand scope of what we're talking about.

The only way people know of *any* ancient literature is by way of *copies*, not originals. That's not only true of the Bible; it's true of virtually everything else. And because we're dealing with writings that are so extremely old, you can imagine how few of these manuscripts are likely to have survived into modern times. Here's a list, for example, of a few well-known works from antiquity, including the approximate date of their writing and the number of manuscripts currently on hand.[3]

- Works of the Roman historian Tacitus. First century. Manuscripts: 3.
- *The History of Rome* by Velleius Paterculus. First century. Manuscripts: 1.
- *The Institutes by Gaius*. Second century. Manuscripts: 3.
- *The Jewish War* by Josephus. First century. Manuscripts: 50.

Fifty—wow! That's quite a jump from the others, isn't it? But as you can see, that number is fairly unusual for writings this old. In almost every case even the most widely accepted works from ancient philosophers and historians are considered verifiable with only a small handful of available sources to vouch for them.

So are you ready now for the number of surviving manuscripts from the New Testament that we know about and can currently access?

We'll give you a hint: it's way more than fifty.

Try more like fifty-eight hundred. And if you add Latin, you have over eight thousand more.

And that doesn't include a vast number of *citations*—places where Christian teachers of the first centuries AD, quoting directly from Scripture in their own writings, provide even *more* evidence of what the earliest documents of the Bible actually said. Even someone like Bart Ehrman has admitted that if all of these secondhand quotes were compiled and cataloged in biblical order, laid from end to end, they would be "sufficient alone for the reconstruction of practically the entire New Testament."[4]

So, the amount of available biblical manuscripts? Plus citations? Huge. The Bible is *by far* the best-attested book of ancient origin.

Yet with some folks even fifty-eight hundred aren't enough. It is hard to know what would qualify. Maybe if we had more early manuscripts (most of the ones we have are later manuscripts). But we have to recall that these works were written on materials that wear out. You made copies because earlier copies got old and became brittle or just plain unusable.

It's almost like somebody walking into the Library of Congress and asking if these are all the books they've got.

In fact, Ehrman was asked once in a debate forum, "How much evidence *would* be enough for you to trust the reliability of the New Testament?" His answer? "Well, if we had early copies, if we had copies of Mark. . . . Suppose next week, there is an archaeological find in Egypt, say, it's in Rome, an archaeological find in Rome, and we have reason to think that these ten manuscripts that are discovered were all copied within a week of the original copy of Mark, and they disagree in 0.001% of their textual variation, then I would say, that's good evidence, and that's precisely what we don't have."[5]

Is it realistic to expect this of any ancient work and its manuscript evidence? This is a standard applied nowhere else in dealing with ancient texts. It is a skewed expectation. After all, papyri wear out. You had to make new copies to preserve the text.

It appears, then, the issue is not really about the presence of sufficient material. As one of us has stated in a previous work, "The bar always seems to be set just a bit higher than wherever the evidence happens to be—like the Greek myth of Sisyphus who thought he had finally done enough to push the boulder to the top of the hill only to find it rolled back down again."[6]

So, how do you answer claims that the Bible is so full of everything from typos to intentional tampering that we can't trust it?

Cleanup in Aisle 5,800

The naysayers are right. Like we said, we don't have the actual, physical documents that Matthew, Mark, Luke, John, and others wrote with their own hand. Can't argue with that. But here's a good place to drag out our sound logic again. Think through this question: *Why does not having the physical originals mean we absolutely CANNOT know with any confidence what the originals said?*

Imagine your mom called to you from the kitchen one evening and said to go tell your little brother and sister, that supper will be ready in fifteen minutes, that one of them needs to set the table and the other one needs to put ice in the glasses. So you get up from whatever you're doing, you walk upstairs, you stand in the hallway where they can both hear you in their rooms, and you say, "Hey, guys, Mom says supper is in fifteen minutes. She wants one of you to set the table and one of you to put ice in the glasses."

All right, did your mom give them these instructions herself? No.

But is that what your mom told you to tell them? Yes.

So, is it possible, even if you're not able to produce an original document with the original information written by the original author, you can still know what the original said with reasonable certainty? Ask the younger siblings in this little example. And see if everybody doesn't come down for supper.

But let's get a little more technical than that. Remember back when we were talking just a few minutes ago about the number of manuscripts that have been preserved from ancient literature? Another way to look at this data is to try determining *how old* the surviving copies are and then subtract their distance in years (or centuries) from when the originals were thought to have been written. The smaller the chronological gap, you'd think, between original and earliest known copy, the higher the likelihood that the first manuscript in our possession reflects what was originally said. Make sense?

So let's look at those same examples again, this time by dating the oldest manuscripts on file, and then subtracting to determine how far apart these copies are from the original.

- Tacitus. Earliest copy: ninth century (800 years after originally written)
- Gaius's *Institutes*. Earliest copy: fifth century (300 years)
- *The Jewish War*. Earliest copy: tenth century or later (900 years)[7]

See the customary time gap we're dealing with? Eight hundred years, nine hundred years—three hundred at the extreme outside. An important thing to remember is that when it comes to these other works, ancient historians work with these copies and discuss history based on their wording. Despite how few manuscripts we have and how large the gap is we still work with these texts. And yet when we get around to the Bible, not only does it far outweigh everything else on the manuscript count— by hundreds and thousands—it also blows away this test on chronological spacing as well.

The New Testament was written, most scholars agree, between AD 50 (if not earlier, in the case of the book of James) and about AD 100 (Revelation). And our earliest fragment—the

John Rylands Papyrus—is a portion of John's Gospel which dates from . . . ready?

Approximately AD 125.

That's hardly a generation later.

Twenty or thirty years. Compared to gaping hundreds! Now, in fairness, this is only a snippet of parts of just a few verses, but it is there, showing us that John's Gospel was written quite early.

And what's more, by the second, third, and fourth centuries, the number of verifiable biblical manuscripts just explodes. Whole sections. Whole books. Our earliest *complete* manuscript of the New Testament—known as Codex Sinaiticus—can be dated to the latter part of that range, sometime in the fourth century.[8]

Again, the wealth of available material is not even in the same league as other writings from that period. Nowhere close. It's everything the historians could want, relatively speaking. At least let's admit it's far, far greater than the sample size of any comparable writing from that era. The many available manuscripts, standing at such close proximity to the originals, offer a windfall of material that scholars who study other ancient works would give a few letters off their Ph.Ds. to obtain.

If they can't have the original, what they want are as many manuscripts as possible so they can compare readings and look for both consistencies and inconsistencies, helping them deduce what the original almost certainly said. And nothing does that like the ancient records of Scripture.

Nothing.

So when you consider the large amount of biblical copying that was being done at the time, as well as the close proximity between the original writings (known as *autographs*) and the earliest known manuscripts, why are we forced to conclude that the copies are so measurably different from where they started? Or that they're any different at all?

Ehrman, for his part, looks at this relative finger snap of a time gap between original and manuscript and asks, Who knows what happened in the interim?[9] Who knows what shenanigans got jumbled up into those few dark decades of history, enough that the complete original was totally corrupted? (Note again the underlying mind-set of doubt.)

Here's what would need to happen to make that accusation true. A scribe in the late first century or early second would need to make wholesale changes to, let's say, the Gospel of Mark. (Just go with it.) And then somehow he would need to ensure that his work replaced every other copy of Mark that had previously been made or was currently being made so that by the time we look at a complete version from the third or fourth century, there's hardly anything recognizable from the original autograph any more. And no trace of the changes shows itself by comparing the earliest manuscripts to one another.[10]

Really?

That is some serious espionage going on. In every biblical book and letter. By a consortium of conspirators swooping down on every little dwelling where any kind of copying was taking place. It is far more likely that what we have reaches back into the early period. The manuscripts we have come from a variety of regions and a variety of times. The pool of manuscripts is so large that it likely reflects a genuine history of copying touching on the originals.

So when scholars assert the likelihood of wholesale changes of a now lost original, they're making what's known as an *argument from silence*—not an appeal to proof and reason and historical documentation but just an imaginary game of connect-the-dots—with no dots and no pencil.

See what a massive leap it takes to get there?

This is unduly skeptical. With no original, the claim is, there's no telling. The check to this claim is in the manuscripts we do have.

With all these copies to work from, and with their nearness to the approximate date of authorship, the most *likely* conclusion is this: *even with a number of changes embedded here and there within the various manuscripts*—whether by mistake or by intention—*the original wording is still present within the full body of material.*

It would be like if you made fifty photocopies of this two-page spread you're reading right now, and you gave one each to fifty different people, along with a Sharpie pen and these instructions: *Cross out one word on each page—any word—and give the sheet back to me.* By the time you reassembled all fifty pages, what are the chances that the same word would have been marked through fifty times by fifty people? Almost none, right? The most logical hypothesis would say that every single word on these two pages would still be discoverable by comparing all fifty of these slightly marred papers against the others.

That's how you get back to the original—even with mistakes potentially present in *all* the manuscripts individually. And that's why the more manuscripts you can access, the greater your confidence that you can locate the original wording. Otherwise, it's like the old joke that says if you have two watches, you don't really know *for sure* what time it is. The chances of both of them being on the same minute and second at the same moment is pretty slight. But if you had a hundred watches, a thousand watches—fifty-eight hundred watches—you could get really, really close to the exact time. If not right on it.

This is the kind of work that's done by an entire field of research and study we already identified as *textual criticism*.[11] (That, incidentally, is Ehrman's original occupation; he's a text critic.) Keep your radar up for this term because it's one you're likely to hear a lot in your college courses on the Bible and religion, as well as in PBS documentaries and *TIME* magazine articles. The true job of the biblical text critic is to analyze this unusual wealth of ancient information and to try to determine, by comparing the available materials against one another, what the original documents of Scripture most likely said.

As a result, with all these manuscripts to work from, what we have is not a loss of the original but just a thin, added layer of inconsistencies—differences in wording or spelling or sentence structure—what scholars refer to as *variants*. In other words we have *too much* of the text, not *too little*, to sift out the authentic from the unauthentic. We might even say that instead of having less than *100 percent* of the Bible text, we have more like *105 percent*. We haven't completely lost the original portion; to the contrary, it is more reasonable to conclude that we have the original and then a little more. It just takes a little dusting and sweeping to clean up the extra scraps and get it back like it was.

We don't have the original manuscripts, they say, so we can't know what the original manuscripts said. Sounds sensible when they say it. But not when you really think about it, especially in light of the many copies we do have.

Of Mountains and Molehills

Please be sure you don't hear us saying that any variants (differences) across manuscripts are contrived by biblical critics or don't matter to biblical students. They do exist, and they are worth our concern. Determining what the original writings actually said is a justifiably important exercise. Good for those who point out these things.

But they're mistaken to give the impression that, depending on which reading is chosen as authentic, we're looking at a big change in who the Bible says Jesus is, what he said, or how we're instructed to live and believe as a result. Even if we decided generally to agree with the skeptics on their own pet renderings of Scripture, the results still wouldn't throw the Bible out of consistency with itself. Keep reading and you'll see.

Here, for example, is how Ehrman introduces what he considers the most significant variants under discussion, all the while claiming "the very meaning of the text is at stake, depending on how one resolves a textual problem":

> Was Jesus an angry man [Mark 1:41]? Was
> he completely distraught in the face of death
> [Heb. 2:8–9]? Did he tell his disciples that
> they could drink poison without being harmed
> [Mark 16:9–20]? Did he let an adulteress off
> the hook with nothing but a mild warning

> [John 7:53–8:11]? Is the doctrine of the
> Trinity explicitly taught in the New Testament
> [1 John 5:7–8]? Is Jesus actually called "the
> unique God" there [John 1:18]? Does the New
> Testament indicate that even the Son of God
> himself does not know when the end will come
> [Matt. 24:36]? The questions go on and on,
> and all of them are related to how one resolves
> difficulties in the manuscript tradition as it has
> come down to us.[12]

But whatever small, isolated phrases of meaning might still be in question, they're still basically like bugs in your car grille. You see them, you know they create a tiny bit of mess, you know they could use some washing, but they don't slow down your forward momentum *at all*, any more than these so-called "major" problems deflect the speeding train of biblical theology even a fraction of an inch.

So just what is at stake in some of these different readings? Let's play being a textual critic for a little while.

Let's look quickly at these seven so-called biggies Ehrman mentions in that inset paragraph. We'll start with the examples where we agree with Ehrman.

Variants 1, 2, and 3—Mark 16:9–20; John 7:53–8:11; 1 John 5:7–8

In these three cases almost all scholars on every side of the spectrum are in full agreement. No argument whatsoever! Check it out in your own Bible, and you'll see that the Mark and John passages are almost guaranteed to be bracketed off with a textual note somewhere saying these are *not* found in the earliest biblical manuscripts, that they don't seem original. And in the 1 John case the variant that adds a summarized explanation of the Trinity—"For there are three that testify in heaven: the Father, the word, and the Holy Spirit, and these three are One"—probably doesn't show up in your Bible at all. If it's anywhere, it's down in the footnotes saying that it doesn't appear in the earliest manuscripts, that it's not original.

So let's peel those three away from the seven. Almost nobody accepts these verses as being authentic to the Gospels or letters. So to adduce these as evidence of corruption in modern versions of the Bible is essentially to carry on a conversation within one's own head, not with most Christian scholars. If anything, these are actually good, healthy examples of exactly what we've been talking about: how the abundance of manuscripts helps us narrow down the original wordings of the Bible. Again, for any serious scholar to cite any or all of these three examples as evidence that the text on which our Bibles are based is corrupt is downright disingenuous. He should know better. He does know better.

Now here is an important question to consider given the agreement on these three examples. In light of these texts not being original, what do we lose overall in what the Bible teaches? The answer is: nothing! The only thing that changes are how many texts in the Bible teach a certain idea. The Bible still teaches Jesus rose from the dead, that he emphasized the grace of forgiveness, and that God involves the Father, Son, and Spirit.

Variant 4—Mark 1:41

This verse describes Jesus healing a leper. And your Bible probably says he did so because he was "moved with compassion." A few of the manuscripts, however, indicate he was motivated by something else—*anger*. Which is obviously different from compassion. Which is it, anger or compassion? Do we have the major problem at hand here that Ehrman alleges? Not even close. Consider that even if "anger" were correct, it wouldn't be the only case where Jesus showed anger (such as when clearing the temple or rebuking the Pharisees). Besides, the Bible in no way equates all anger with being wrong. In fact, Psalm 4:4, which Paul picked up and repeated in Ephesians 4:26, says, "Be angry and do not sin." So no matter which reading is adopted in Mark 1, Jesus' infallible life is not in danger. Could Jesus be angry and still be God? Of course he could. And whether or not Mark 1:41 says he was angry, other places say he was angry about other stuff at other times. In fact, if we asked what Jesus was angry about here, it would be at the fallen human condition in a damaged creation that leads to leprosy and the need for healing. It would be an anger that has an element of compassion in it! So what's the big problem here?

Variant 5—Hebrews 2:8–9

In some manuscript copies these verses describe Jesus as dying "apart from God" rather than what your Bible translation likely says "by God's grace." And, yes, the second rendering doesn't come off sounding quite as distraught as the first. But the fact that Jesus' death was agonizing to him on a human level is consistent with the other teaching of Scripture. So as

Dan Wallace has said, "If this is the view of Jesus throughout Hebrews, how does the variant that Ehrman adopts in 2:9 change that portrait?"[13] It doesn't. When Jesus from the cross cited Psalm 22:1 about God forsaking him, Jesus was making the same point. The only issue becomes how many different passages make that point.

Variant 6—John 1:18

This verse refers to Jesus as the "One and Only Son," but a significant variant switches out the word "Son" for "God." Either reading, however, still fits consistently within John's message and within the rest of the New Testament. John opens and closes his Gospel with testimony to Jesus being *God* (John 1:1; 20:28). And similarly, the well-known John 3:16 is but one of a great number of examples where he documents Jesus' identity as God's unique *Son*. So again, there's no theological problem here between "One and Only Son" and "One and Only God."[14] John's testimony to Jesus' deity doesn't depend on this one variant. It's secure no matter how the passage reads.

Variant 7—Matthew 24:36

This verse records Jesus telling his disciples that he didn't know the "day and hour" when the end would occur—a statement also recorded in Mark 13:32. If someone wants to disapprove of Jesus saying this, if they don't see why he should have been unaware while he was ministering on earth of when his return would be, that's a separate issue to debate altogether. But it really has nothing to do with whether this wording is original.

Claims that variants like these show that the copies of the Bible are full of mistakes go too far. We know what the options are and that the original is somewhere in the choice. So what have we really lost?

Not much. If anything. We simply discuss which meaning was and is original with an awareness that the other reading might be such. We also do so aware that if this specific passage does not teach this idea, it likely does show up somewhere else in Scripture.

What Big Eyes You Have

Bart Ehrman puts the number of active, questionable variants in the New Testament at somewhere between 200,000 and 400,000—which, again, makes for some spicy ad copy. *Just look at all the unknowns and unknowables in your Bible!*

But what drains all the color from these in-your-face statistics is the simple math of what happens when fifty-eight hundred manuscripts are available to be laid down for comparison, as opposed to just two or three. It's the same reason Cy Young—who will forever hold the all-time record for career wins as a Major League baseball pitcher (511)—also holds the all-time record for something else: career *losses*. You know why? Because of another baseball record he holds: he pitched a thousand innings more than any other player in baseball history.

The more manuscripts, the more variants.

Scholar and author Mark Roberts provides a mathematical illustration:

This book [referring to the one his quote is
from] has almost 50,000 words. Suppose I
asked two people to make copies of this book
by hand. Suppose, further, that they made one
mistake every 1,000 words (99.9% accuracy).
When they finished, each of their manuscripts
would have 50 mistakes, for a total of 100. This
doesn't sound too bad, does it? But suppose
I asked 2,000 people to make copies of my
book. And suppose they also made a mistake
every 1,000 words. When they finished, the
total of mistakes in their manuscripts would be
100,000. This sounds like a lot of variants—
more than the words in my book, Bart Ehrman
would say. But in fact the large number of variants is a simple product of the large number of
manuscripts.[15]

Possessing more manuscripts of ancient literature should
be nothing but a positive. *Never* a negative. Any fair-minded
historian would agree with that. Only an excessive skepticism
turns a benefit into a problem. That move is neither necessary
nor reasonable.

Besides, the overwhelming number of variants—and we
mean all but a very, very, *very* small amount—are as minor as
minor can be and for the most part are exceedingly easy to spot
and discount. They consist of things like simple spelling errors,
flip-flops in word order, nonsense readings that are obviously
the result of tired eyes and a lack of concentration. Ehrman
himself says, "To be sure, of all the hundreds of thousands of

textual changes found among our manuscripts, most of them are completely insignificant, immaterial, and of no real importance of anything other than showing the scribes could not spell or keep focused any better than the rest of us."[16]

There you go.

But if most all of these variants are as insignificant as he says—as they are—then why give the impression there's such a big problem?

Best Business Practices

So you see what we're talking about? The seemingly shocking sound bites comes from the skeptical camp really distort the big picture on this issue. The next challenge some raise is with the whole business model that birthed the manuscript copying trade.

Some people would have you believe the early Christian scribal community was kind of like the Wild West—no infrastructure, no norms, no organization—pure freelance and freewheeling. They'll tell you the scribes who copied the texts were amateurs, unreliable, sometimes even illiterate, making up the rules as they went along. No wonder their manuscripts are so full of mistakes, they say.

Let us counter that claim with a few terms that give evidence to the contrary—brought to you by the letters M, N, and C, and by the number three: (1) *multifunctional scribes*, (2) *nomina sacra*, and (3) *codex*.

Exhibit 1—Multifunctional Scribes

The handwriting found in the earliest Christian manuscripts indicates these documents were not the work of one-tool, literary scribes whose primary job was copying books for commercial sale. Rather they seem to have been created by professionals who were employed by individuals for their skill in many areas, such as copying letters, taking dictation, generating administrative documents, and reproducing formal literary pieces.[17] These *multifunctional scribes* were prevalent in the first century—like Tertius, for example, mentioned by name as the individual who took down Paul's letter to the Romans (see Rom. 16:22). What's more, "There is no reason to think that commercially produced books were of higher quality than privately made copies," writes Harry Gamble in a study on early Christian texts. "Indeed, frequent complaints suggest they were often worse."[18]

Exhibit 2—Nomina Sacra

In response to the notion that individual scribes routinely concocted their own style and formatting preferences, we present to you the conventional practice known as *nomina sacra*—a code of standard abbreviations for special words such as *Jesus*, *Christ*, *Lord*, and *God*. You may think it just a primitive form of shorthand, an attempt to save space and ink. But the Greek language contained many common words that were much longer than these, words that would've made equal or better sense to shorten. The words that were chosen for this treatment, however, were those with divine significance, which tells us the scribes likely handled them this way to express reverence and devotion. But even if not, (1) these abbreviations do appear consistently in the earliest manuscripts, (2) they were exclusive to Christianity, and (3) they're seen among widespread regions and languages. So evidence suggests the early scribes were not all freestyle independents but rather had a "degree of organization, of conscious planning, and uniformity of practice."[19]

Exhibit 3—Codex

The primary vehicle for reading and correspondence during the first centuries AD was the scroll, which was rolled out to be read, then rolled up again to be stored. But Christians preferred the *codex* for their collection of Scripture—a binding of papyrus or parchment that looked more like our modern-day books. While the culture at large wouldn't gravitate toward the codex until sometime in the fourth century (similar to our migration from CDs to MP3s), this platform was already common practice for the Christians by the end of the *second* century. The most likely reason is because the codex could hold more than one book, bound together, which is exactly what the Bible was and is. It indicates a mentality that understood these books belonged together and they were to be held in high regard. But it definitely reveals "a Christian scribal culture that is quite unified, organized, and able to forge a new literary path by employing a revolutionary book technology that would eventually come to dominate the entire Greco-Roman world."[20] That's why Christians *uniformly* used the codex rather than the scroll—no diversity here.

Bottom line, while gaps certainly remain in our understanding of the ancient copying process—same as for all other subsets of ancient history—those people who were involved in the transmission of Christian texts appear less like a gang of lawless loners and more like a developing colony with guidelines and standards and organized practices—and therefore not a breeding ground for sloppy work and runaway writing mistakes.

The Power of Words

No matter what we say, the upshot of this manuscript corruption scandal—overplayed though it is—basically comes down to this for Bart Ehrman: "How does it help us to say that the Bible is the inerrant word of God if in fact we don't have the words that God inerrantly inspired, but only the words copied by the scribes—sometimes correctly but sometimes (many times!) incorrectly?[21] . . . If God really wanted people to have his actual words, surely he would have miraculously preserved those words, just as he had miraculously inspired them in the first place. Given that he didn't preserve the words, the conclusion must be that he hadn't gone to the trouble of inspiring them."[22]

What a statement. If taken at face value while you're furiously scribbling it down in your lecture notes, it can feel like the final word. You take it on the chin and you move on. He's right. What else can you do? Who can argue with that?

But as we've been saying, it's not as ironclad as it seems.

Except for the first scribes who worked directly from the autographs, none of the others throughout history were physically engaging with the actual, *material* words of Paul or John or Peter. Neither are you. Neither are we. But words obviously possess an *immaterial* quality as well. They're larger than print and ink or even papyrus and parchment.

The words we're writing at this moment, for example, were first composed in our individual minds, then punched into a keyboard, where they took shape on a screen, then were saved as electronic data, then sent wirelessly to the publisher, then printed into this book (along with, we hope, hundreds and thousands of other copies)! And yet these words are *still* not finished working. They're communicating information to you and to other readers right at this moment, who might repeat those same words to a parent or quote them in a paper or recall them later when your faith is being challenged.

Words are alive. They keep going.

As author and lecturer Peter Williams has said, "Words do not lose inspiration by being copied."[23] So if by working through the wide assortment of surviving manuscripts, we can reasonably deduce that what we're looking at in our Bibles are genuine replicas and translations of the original sources, then why are these words so suspiciously second-rate, just because God didn't keep the first ones—the first parchments—under glass in the archives?

In fact, Bart Ehrman's statement quoted above about the inspiration of the Bible (or lack thereof) is based on a fallacious understanding of the doctrine of inspiration. Christians believe the *words* written in the original autographs were inspired, not the *material entity* (the specific piece of papyrus or parchment). Therefore, we don't need the original *manuscript* in order to have the original *words*.

Again, a textual critic can certainly prove the point that particular manuscripts have been altered in a number of places. Anyone worth his scholarly salt would agree. But no way can they demonstrate how, among the thousands of manuscripts we can study and research and access through our biblical software, the original words of Scripture have utterly vanished. Gone.

All these corruption arguments, when you dig all the way down to their roots, are actually "have your cake and eat it too" affairs. On the one hand the people who cling to them insist that nobody can know for sure what was actually contained in the initial autographs. *Show me one*, they say, *and then we'll talk.* But then they confidently argue how these numerous variants—this one, that one, and the other one—couldn't possibly be original to the text. Well, how can they know this to be true if they don't have any idea what the original said? How do we know a watch is not a Rolex unless we know what a Rolex is—and believe that Rolex watches exist?

Talk about inconsistencies.

Ehrman, for example, has written a book entitled *Did Jesus Exist?* in which he rightly defends the historical existence of Jesus, despite casting him as a confused idealist, a tragic figure losing a bold gamble with fate. Yet many of Ehrman's arguments in the book are based on the words of Jesus in the New Testament, meaning he must possess at least *some* confidence in the biblical text and its safe transmission across the years.

Strange how some skeptics can be so *assured* of things like motives in the long-deceased mind of a second-century scribe, about whom they know nothing except what his handwriting may have looked like. Yet they can remain so *unconvinced* at what hundreds of ancient manuscripts offer as physical evidence for what the original Bible text said—manuscripts they could pull up and view on their computer tablets at home this very night.

So just pocket that one away in your hard drive—how the skepticism some people may attach to your reasonable defense of Scripture is often contrasted by their own certainty that they know what you cannot. After all, "reasonable" is as far as you should be asked to drive your argument. Whenever dealing with ancient history, such as the integrity of the biblical text and its transmission—things that cannot be investigated with personal interviews and primary research—the question before the secular classroom is not so much if we can have *absolute* certainty but *sufficient* certainty.

Can we trust with sufficient reason that we have access to the text of the Bible? The answer to this question is simply yes.

Discussion Questions

1. How do scholars determine the original words of the New Testament?
2. How does the New Testament manuscript evidence compare to the evidence for other books written in the first century?
3. Why are there so many differences in the manuscripts of the New Testament?
4. Can anyone prove we do not have the original words of the New Testament? Why or why not?

6

And the Winner Is . . .

Who Decided What Christianity Was Made Of?

There were lots of early Christian groups. They all claimed to be right. They all had books to back up their claims, books allegedly written by the apostles and therefore representing the views of Jesus and his first disciples. The group that won out did not represent the teachings of Jesus or his apostles. . . . The victorious group called itself orthodox. But it was not the original form of Christianity, and it won its victory only after many hard-fought battles.
—Bart Ehrman[1]

In the beginning was Diversity. And the Diversity was with God, and the Diversity was God. Without Diversity was nothing made that was made. And it came to pass that nasty old "orthodox" people narrowed down diversity and finally squeezed it out, dismissing it as heresy. But in the fullness of time (which is of course our time), Diversity rose up and smote orthodoxy hip and thigh. Now, praise be, the only heresy is orthodoxy. As widely and as unthinkably accepted as this recon-struction is, it is historical nonsense: the emperor has no clothes.
—D. A. Carson[2]

Jesus came.
Jesus lived.
Jesus died.
Jesus lives again.

That is the heart of the Christian message.

But is that what Christians have always believed—all the way back to the beginning? The things you experience from wherever you sit on Sunday morning, the things you hear taught and proclaimed from the platform, the things you've been led to believe about God from your pastors and the Scriptures—how do you know this Christian faith is real and authentic?

You know your parents grew up hearing it. Perhaps your grandparents did too. But beyond that, before their time—back as long as people have been worshipping together—is this what Christians were being told? Is this what the church was about? Has this *always* been what God's people have believed?

Or not?

You may likely hear on television or read in a book that the roots of historic Christianity (we're talking about the first, second, third, fourth centuries AD) were basically a tangled mess of competing belief systems. Nobody really knew what Christianity was and stood for. Bart Ehrman says there was no such *thing* as Christianity—in the singular—during the early centuries of our age. Only *Christianities*, in the plural. No uniform, coherent, widely agreed-upon set of beliefs but only a variety of views, none of which could legitimately claim to represent true, authentic Christianity. It wasn't until the political shake-ups of later centuries, he says, that the core truths of what we'd call Christianity would surface as the dominant force, the alpha male, among all others.

To hear them talk, it was sort of like March Madness, a free-for-all, ongoing battles between opposing teams, beating up on each other through the brackets, until one stood alone in that "one shining moment," tearing down the nets of victory. *We win! Take that!*

And say good-bye to all the sweet, cooing sounds of "Kumbaya" Christian diversity. No more big-tent enjoyment of your personally preferred Christian flavor, doing your own thing with all the anything-goes privileges of full acceptance. No more plurality of Christian beliefs. Big Brother wins. Just like big business, big oil . . .

Therefore (the skeptics say), the reason Christianity looks the way it does today, the reason the Bible teaches what it does, the reason we sit in our churches on Sunday and call this particular brand of belief "Christian faith" is only because this is *the side that won*. It could have just as easily gone another direction.

Today's Christianity (the term for it is *orthodoxy*) was ultimately hashed out in highbrow, heavy-handed meeting rooms of a later era, not simply through a Man, a cross, an empty tomb, and his personally commissioned disciples. The real shapers of orthodoxy came along in the third and fourth centuries, they say, seizing the opportunity for dominance when it presented itself, rewriting history to make it appear as if theirs (ours) was the only legitimate form of Christian belief that ever existed.[3]

Bullies. Strategists. Power brokers. Doing away with their competition. Sweeping any trace of diversity under the rug. Our way or the highway.

And that's where Christianity came from.

In other words, the skeptics have a conspiracy theory. The splashy story. High intrigue. They know when lecturing in the standard college classroom, who *wouldn't* love to pin the whole notion of Christianity on a bunch of backroom bishops and politicians?

But they've got a big problem in their attempt to divorce Christianity from its immediate connection to Christ's life and teachings, as well as from the apostles and the early church leaders who lived it, in many cases died for it, and shepherded it through their generations. Such cynical views don't stand up well against the evidence. As with the last chapter on biblical transmission, the skeptics' story does make for some hot copy. It feeds into today's postmodern rebellion against authority and absolutes. But in many ways it owes more to their own ideological commitment to *diversity* than to responsible, verifiable *research*. They claim the Bible rose up in later centuries, declared itself the Christian right, and said everybody else was wrong—when the only thing anybody else wanted was just to get along.

This chapter you're about to read goes back in time to show you this is simply not the case, to show you what the faith traditions of *your church* and the *early church* had in common, to show you why Christian faith has *always* been the Christian faith.

Bully Pulpit

Many of the skeptical opinions concerning the origins of Christian belief stem from the work of Walter Bauer, an early twentieth-century scholar whose book *Heresy and Orthodoxy in*

Earliest Christianity (published in 1934) crystallized the view that Christianity was at heart a power grab. He argued that heresy (meaning any teaching that deviates from standard norms—in this case, teaching that disagrees with modern orthodoxy) was actually the *original form* of Christianity in certain regions of the early world and was at least an established minority nearly everywhere. But by the end of the second century, the Roman church's size and appetite for control had ramrodded competing views off the religious stage, then proceeded to expunge any evidence of these views from the record over the next three or four centuries, cementing their own control over Christendom.

Bart Ehrman has called Bauer's volume the "most important book on the history of early Christianity in the twentieth century" and classifies his stated arguments as "incisive" and "authoritative, made by the master of all the surviving early Christian literature."[4]

Obviously this book has done some major shaping of Ehrman's own views.

But a book whose very title professes to be dealing with "earliest Christianity" should probably focus on the earliest evidence available from history, don't you think?—namely, the first-century New Testament documents themselves. Instead Bauer based his findings almost entirely on documents that date from the second century and later, using these to speculate backwards on the first century, then turning his retroactive guesswork into "authoritative" fact.[5]

So while his book has been shown by many researchers to be "constructive fantasy" and "elegantly worked out fiction,"[6] it still remains foundational to the skeptical viewpoint. And who should be surprised? Skeptics often accept arguments that portray Christianity as muddled, man-made, and manufactured. They have a stake in arguing that the veins of Christian faith don't actually flow directly from Jesus' bloodline. The dispute is important, because if the original Christianity was diverse, no one has the right to claim their version of Christianity is it. That it is the truth. This kind of claim for diversity is attractive because it undercuts the claim there is a truth out there that matters. Where there is diversity, there is no orthodoxy.

This is why the skepic's pull is to try and get you to buy into an early history of diversity.

But they should not get to take you along with them for good historical reasons.

You and Whose Army?

No one disputes that Christianity was filled with controversies in its early days (or still today, for that matter). Theological wildfires are nothing new. We need only look at Paul's letters to the Galatians and Colossians, his pastoral epistles to Timothy and Titus, as well as 2 Peter, 1 John, and Jude, to see that these writings were largely intended to combat heresy (see Gal. 1:6; Col. 2:11–21; 1 Tim. 1:3; Titus 1:5).

But most of the flashpoints the apostles were addressing in the first century—disputes such as whether circumcision was required of Gentile believers—do not touch on the core debates of orthodoxy that would later arise.[7] When you hear talk about offshoot Christian sects that developed in early days—such as the Gnostics, the Docetists, and the Marcionites—these groups cannot be dated from historical sources before the second century. Just can't.[8] We have no evidence to support the argument that all of this significant diversity was happening right off the bat.

Second century? Third century? Fourth century? Even then, the evidence shows orthodoxy as being pervasive and stable throughout that time.[9] Consistently. Across continents. But if, for argument's sake, we were to concede the widespread, burgeoning, equal presence of Christian factions during these later centuries—seeing them almost like our current choice between Methodists, Baptists, and Presbyterians—nothing but pure conjecture can place them at or near the dawn of the early church. And nothing but wishful thinking can portray them as robust alternatives to authentic faith and belief.[10]

Nothing.

Take Gnosticism, for example, which clearly posed the greatest threat to Christianity. We touched on their existence back in chapter 3 in our discussion on the biblical canon and their various writings, like the Gospel of Philip, the Gospel of Mary. And if any heresy should have been high on the watch list, it was this one.

Gnosticism can only be construed as a broad label that covered a wide variety of groups with wildly divergent views. As a general rule Gnostics were highly suspicious of all things physical, including the humanity of Jesus. They also held to the presence of a secret mystical knowledge that set them above the everyday crowd—and, not shockingly, set them apart from one another. Even among the Gnostic camp, agreement was hard to come by. They never developed any organization or unity. No church. No group of churches. No church basketball league. And their writings were never considered *at any time* for inclusion in the New Testament canon, since for one thing their theology denied the legitimacy of the Old Testament. That was a clear nonnegotiable.

Authentic Christianity, on the other hand, was already planting flourishing churches as early as the AD 40s and 50s.[11] And as these churches grew and developed, they increasingly viewed themselves as part of a unified network (what one writer has dubbed a "holy internet"[12]), complete with leadership structures and cooperative interaction.

And with core beliefs. As seen in the New Testament documents, which were written mid-first century, the church was already stressing the importance of holding on to true doctrine and rejecting false teaching. In no uncertain terms! It's hard to read the letters of Paul, for instance, and not see a clear, early body of orthodox beliefs that were up and operational from the get-go.

By the second century this "rule of faith" had successfully bridged the gap between the ministry of the apostles and those who emerged as leaders heading into the next generation—the *church fathers*, we call them (those who were most influential in the years following). Their writings reveal an awareness and affirmation of a commonly held faith, a theological standard that unified a geographically diverse group of post-New Testament churches.[13] They saw themselves as "handing down" what had been entrusted to them by those who had actually walked with Christ.

More than that, the church fathers understood their doctrine as being rooted in the Jewish Scriptures—the Old Testament—tying the church to the truly ancient faith of God's people and the prophetic messages that were fulfilled in Christ and proclaimed by the apostles. They weren't *inventing* a rule of faith; they were *recipients* of it.

Theirs was a legacy of truth. From strength to strength.

And Gnosticism was a toe-to-toe competitor with *that*? *Really?*

If the battle for orthodoxy was truly as evenly contested as some assert, if these heresies legitimately had the numbers and stamina to survive and dominate the Christian landscape, nothing was standing in their way from lacing it up and duking it out. Early Christian orthodoxy had no official authority to suppress what they perceived as heretical teaching. Just the opposite. Their beliefs were highly unpopular in the wider world, always risking the collar of persecution. Often fatally so. Those in the early church weren't clinging to Christ in hopes of attaining social or political power. They did it because they believed this teaching to be true. Because it *was* true. *Is* true.

It wasn't until much later—AD 313, with the sanctioning of the Edict of Milan by Emperor Constantine—that Christians acquired the official means to take action against heretical groups. And by this time Gnosticism had already faded quietly from the scene, all on its own, vanishing into the thin air their beliefs were anchored in, long before orthodox Christianity could pop the balloon for them.

Poof.

Ask anybody who's tried, and they'll tell you: it's hard to get an organization off the ground, to find enough people who believe in what you're saying, who'll take a chance on hitching their wagon to your plan and potential. So when we take a view of the second-, third-, and fourth-century world and see Christian orthodoxy thriving and see heresies like Gnosticism sputtering, what does that tell you? Who was most likely the parasite of whom? Amid all this apparent (or imagined) diversity, who was marching boldly ahead, and who was off to the side?

The battle for Christianity's public face was not a tug-of-war among equals. These opponents did produce enough of a stir to worry orthodox writers for a time. But they eventually faded away, in part because of the endorsement of social and political forces Constantine launched, but also because they lacked the early and strong roots that orthodoxy had.

Growing Strong from the Ground Up

According to the critics of Christianity, the centuries between Christ's disappearance from the scene and the official construction of the Bible was just a big, syrupy mess of uncongealed thinking and beliefs. So naturally it was going to take people some time to figure out how to put all these things together in their minds.

That's what they'd have you believe.

But that's not what the Scriptures say. When we appeal here to the Scriptures, it is not just because it is the Bible that we cite these texts. These are the first-century witnesses we possess that tell us what people of the faith believed. These texts are our only windows into the earliest Christianity in terms of historical sources. They take us as far back as we can go. As we've been hinting and explaining in this chapter, the New Testament authors—whose work is verified by hundreds of early manuscripts—reveal extremely defined understandings about Jesus, his identity, his mission, and his purpose for the church, right from the beginning.

We present the following Bible passages as evidence. Any skeptic can certainly choose on a personal level not to believe what these verses say. But they can hardly deny that these Scriptures do reflect what the early Christians affirmed and believed themselves.

The Gospels and Acts

> Simon Peter answered, "You are the Messiah, the Son of the living God!" And Jesus responded, "Simon son of Jonah, you are blessed because flesh and blood did not reveal this to you, but My Father in heaven. And I also say to you that you are Peter, and on this rock I will build My church, and the forces of Hades will not overpower it." (Matt. 16:16–18)

> Then Jesus came near and said to them, "All authority has been given to Me in heaven and on earth. Go, therefore, and make disciples of all nations, baptizing them in the name of the Father and of the Son and of the Holy Spirit, teaching them to observe everything I have

commanded you. And remember, I am with you always, to the end of the age." (Matt. 28:18–20)

And they devoted themselves to the apostles' teaching, to the fellowship, to the breaking of bread, and to the prayers. (Acts 2:42)

Paul

I am amazed that you are so quickly turning away from Him who called you by the grace of Christ and are turning to a different gospel—not that there is another gospel, but there are some who are troubling you and want to change the good news about the Messiah. But even if we or an angel from heaven should preach to you a gospel other than what we have preached to you, a curse be on him! As we have said before, I now say again: If anyone preaches to you a gospel contrary to what you received, a curse be on him! (Gal. 1:6–9)

Now I want you to know, brothers, that the gospel preached by me is not based on human thought. For I did not receive it from a human source and I was not taught it, but it came by a revelation from Jesus Christ. (Gal. 1:11–12)

Therefore, brothers, stand firm and hold to the traditions you were taught, either by our message or by our letter. (2 Thess. 2:15)

Now I urge you, brothers, to watch out for those who cause dissensions and obstacles contrary to the doctrine you have learned. Avoid them. (Rom. 16:17)

As I urged you when I went to Macedonia, remain in Ephesus so that you may instruct certain people not to teach different doctrine. (1 Tim. 1:3)

Hold on to the pattern of sound teaching that you have heard from me, in the faith and love that are in Christ Jesus. Guard, through the Holy Spirit who lives in us, that good thing entrusted to you. (2 Tim. 1:13–14)

Jude and John

Dear friends, although I was eager to write you about the salvation we share, I found it necessary to write and exhort you to contend for the faith that was delivered to the saints once for all. (Jude 3)

Dear friends, do not believe every spirit, but test the spirits to determine if they are from God, because many false prophets have gone

out into the world. This is how you know the
Spirit of God: Every spirit who confesses that
Jesus Christ has come in the flesh is from God.
(1 John 4:1–2)

You want more? We could give you more.

Several doctrinal summaries that appear in the New
Testament proved foundational to the early church in clarifying
overall beliefs (Rom. 1:2–4; 1 Cor. 8:4–6; 11:23–25; 15:3–6; and
many others). First-generation Christians were able to use these
as a way of conveying truth among themselves, even before a
usable collection of Scriptures existed. A number of other passages appear to be almost like hymns, a way of helping solidify
core doctrine (Col. 1:15–20; Phil. 2:6–11; 1 Tim. 3:16).

(Did you know, by the way, that the hymns of the church
throughout history were intended primarily for that purpose—
to teach and reinforce sound doctrine in a memorable form?
Before we started putting the words up on big screens, the
church maintained their songs in hymnbooks. And if you'll go
back and look at one of these hymnals, you'll see how each song
often communicated a complete doctrinal statement, usually a
complete retelling of the gospel in capsule. These songs weren't
just to dance to. They were to learn from. This was the understood meaning and method of hymns for centuries and was
particularly true at the dawn of the church.)

But even that wasn't all. Early Christians also had the sacra-
ments of baptism and the Lord's Supper to help them repeatedly
witness and rehearse the tenets of their faith, not to mention having the enormous bank of teaching available to them

through the Hebrew Scriptures, which were already prevalent at that time.

So we ask you: No standards in place? No knowledge of what they believed? Is that what somebody said?

By any measure the New Testament paints a much different portrait than those who say early Christianity lacked benchmarks for how to weed out true teaching from false teaching. Look again at some of those verses we gave you. Notice . . .

- The apostles knew their mission was to pass on Jesus' message to subsequent generations.
- The church understood the importance of being faithful to the apostles' teaching.
- The core message of the gospel was tied to the nature and work of Christ.

It's everywhere. And authoritative. And early.

And it wasn't to be messed with. Even the apostle Paul, clearly the most towering figure in early Christianity, didn't consider himself free to tweak the divine message he had received. Pull up Galatians 1 again: "Even if we or an angel from heaven should preach to you a gospel other than what we have preached to you, a curse be on him!" If the great Paul himself didn't have the clearance to tamper with the central teaching concerning Jesus' saving death, burial, and resurrection, then surely nobody else did. And anybody who claimed to be Christian and didn't hold to these truths could expect to be challenged. By gospel standards.

His Truth Is Marching On

Bible skeptics insist on imposing an artificially murky distance between the life of Jesus and the establishment of the Christian faith. But let's take a little stroll from the first century to the fourth, noting the ongoing connections from one season to the next. The following exercise serves as an approximate outline of the relationship between orthodoxy and divergent forms of heresy in the first three hundred years of Christianity.[14]

Strap yourself in. Here we go:

AD 33
Jesus dies and rises from the dead.
No later than AD 35, Paul is converted and adopts the church's exalted Christology and teaching on salvation.

40s–60s
Paul writes letters to various churches.
Orthodoxy is pervasive and mainstream.
Churches are organized around a central message.
Undeveloped heresies begin to emerge.
Dispute about how Gentiles come into the church.
Scripture teaches core theology.
Early orthodox writings circulate in the church.

60s–90s
The Gospels and remaining New Testament are written.
These writings continue propagating orthodoxy.
Orthodoxy stays pervasive and mainstream.

Heresies are still undeveloped. Some Jewish groups hold to the law, and a few argue Jesus is something less than God in a position known as adoptionism.
Peter and Paul die in the 60s.

90s–130s
New Testament writers pass from the scene.
The church fathers emerge, cultivating established orthodoxy.
Orthodoxy remains pervasive and mainstream.
Heresies begin to organize—a little.
Gnostic Christianity begins to emerge.

130s–200s
The church fathers begin dying out.
Subsequent Christian writers carry on their mission.
Orthodoxy is still the established norm of Christianity.
Heresies remain subsidiary, scattered, loose, disorganized.
Alternative views emerge with enough presence and concern that more orthodox writers challenge and discuss them.

200s–300s
Orthodoxy is solidified in the creeds.
Various heresies continue to rear their head.
Orthodoxy, however, remains clearly dominant in most regions.
Alternatives continue to draw attention from many orthodox writers as a real presence and concern.

And we'll stop there. As you can see, the AD 300s did witness a significant moment in how Christian orthodoxy was defined. But only in a *technical* sense, not in a *material* sense—not in a way that changed or radicalized the orthodox teaching that had been in force from the founding of the early church. This is where Ehrman and the skeptics make too much of their arguments, implying that orthodoxy was cobbled together late in the game just to crush the opposition.

The only thing new at this juncture in church history was the institution of the *creed*—a capsule summary statement of orthodox doctrine. The first major creed was adopted at the first ever, global gathering of church leaders in Nicea (pronounced "nigh-SEE-uh," located in modern Turkey). Still known and recited today, the Nicene Creed is a composite of belief that when translated is contained within approximately 225 English words.

> We believe in one God, the Father, the Almighty, maker of heaven and earth, of all that is, seen and unseen. We believe in one Lord, Jesus Christ, the only Son of God, eternally begotten of the Father, God from God, light from light, true God from true God, begotten, not made, of one Being with the Father; through him all things were made. For us and for our salvation he came down from heaven, was incarnate of the Holy Spirit and the Virgin Mary and became truly human. For our sake he was crucified under Pontius Pilate; he suffered death and was buried. On the third day he rose again in accordance with the Scriptures; he ascended into heaven and is seated at the right hand of the Father. He will come again in glory

> to judge the living and the dead, and his king-
> dom will have no end. We believe in the Holy
> Spirit, the Lord, the giver of life, who proceeds
> from the Father [and the Son], who with the
> Father and the Son is worshiped and glori-
> fied, who has spoken through the prophets.
> We believe in one holy catholic and apostolic
> Church. We acknowledge one baptism for the
> forgiveness of sins. We look for the resurrec-
> tion of the dead, and the life of the world to
> come.

The Council of Nicea had been summoned to deal with heretical views on the divinity of Christ, a highly philosophical controversy. And as such the heavily belabored wording of the Nicene Creed resulted in phrases intended to recap and clarify what the writings of Peter, Paul, and the Gospel authors had said. The creed does not contain the *words* of Scripture, but its doctrine is clearly *derived* from it, from the long-standing testimony of the New Testament documents.

Wouldn't you say?

But for some reason many skeptics can't track with that. Here is how they make the case. Their arguments imply that if the specific verbiage of the creed didn't come from the mouths and pens of the apostles the creed could therefore not be anything else but a new teaching. Not inspired by God. And what reason would motivate the church of the fourth century to concoct their own brand of Christian belief, call it by the name of orthodoxy, and pretend it went all the way back to Jesus and his original followers? Simple.

Domination. A kick in the teeth of diversity.

One way. Our way.

Black. White.

Yes. No.

Remember again, the council that met at Nicea (and other councils that followed) were not build-a-Bible workshops. They weren't crafting orthodoxy out of thin air. They were dealing with controversies current in their day. Their desire was merely to give fresh, concentrated voice to old teachings in dealing with new, present-day issues. They were expressing the same ideas of Scripture in different words, in a different format. To restrict the wording of the creed to nothing but pinned-together Bible verses would be like saying the only way we can do Bible study today, the only way we can comment biblically on real-world events in our current culture, is exclusively by quoting passages of Scripture verbatim.

But why set such limits?

The biblical canon may be closed, but truth and the Bible are just not that dead.

The creeds appeared amid history as a way of dealing with divergent views, views that *already* existed outside the *already* established boundaries of orthodoxy. By saying the same things in different phrases and wordings, the church was not *replacing* orthodox teaching but only *reapplying* it to specific issues.

Again, the rush to read into these events from church history everything from conspiracy and corruption to scorched-earth propaganda and the rewriting of Scripture does not come from verifiable research. It comes from exaggerating the complexity of the Christian landscape in the first centuries of our era.

That complexity gives a misleading impression of a far greater diversity in the first-century scene than really existed. It tries to level the playing field between alternative forms of Christianity so orthodoxy looks less unique or dominant. It makes the history of Christianity one of a choice between equals.

Give them diversity, it seems, or die. Actually, the argument is: give them diversity, and any truth claim dies.

Faith of Our Fathers

Make no mistake about it, a case can be made about *legitimate* diversity in the Christian faith. Each of us has been given a set of spiritual gifts to exercise, and the Bible calls for unity in diversity. Not everyone is a "leg" or "foot" or "arm." The body needs all of these to function in tandem.

Likewise, in the Bible we have legitimate diversity. Think of the four Gospels, written by four different men, each with their own vocabulary, point of view, and intended audience. As one scholar once remarked, "The music of the New Testament choir is not written to be sung in unison."[15]

But *diversity—legitimate* diversity—doesn't equal *contradiction*. It also doesn't mean lack of a *unifying core*. In our case that unifying core is the gospel, the apostolic teaching about Jesus, who died on the cross for our sins, was buried, was raised on the third day, and will return. That Jesus was raised to share authority over salvation with God and is one to whom all are accountable, offering life in the Spirit to those who accept his gift by faith. The good news is about a journey with God in the context of accepting his forgiveness and the gift of life, both now and for eternity. *That's* the core—call it orthodoxy, if you like—that Paul and the other New Testament writers, in keeping with the Old Testament expectation of a coming Messiah, to a man affirmed. And anybody who didn't—if it was Paul himself, or even an angel from heaven—let a curse be on him.

Don't let anyone fool you, therefore, by moving back and forth between two different kinds of diversity: the kind of legitimate diversity we should celebrate and the diversity that differs on the core beliefs of Christianity. They are miles apart. Worship Jesus each in our own way? Yes, by all means—but only within the parameters of the historic, unifying, first-century Christian gospel.

So you can settle back into your church seat now. This faith of yours—based on Christian doctrines and beliefs you've read and known and embraced—wasn't all cooked up in a committee. It traces all the way back to what people saw and heard and experienced in the physical presence of Jesus. It's real. It's him. It's ageless.

Are there still rivals to orthodox belief today? Yes. People who want to tack Jesus onto heresy? Yes. False teaching? Yes. And the church is commissioned even now, just as it was in its earliest days, to address and expose error, "holding to the faithful message as taught . . . to encourage with sound teaching and to refute those who contradict it" (Titus 1:9).

So we have taken you on a tour to answer legitimate questions people raise about the Christian faith, things you read in books and see on television or read on the Internet. If you have legitimate questions, we hope we have answered them with enough detail that you will think about the profound message the Bible offers about the human condition and your own soul before God.[16] If that message makes sense, feel released to worship. And empowered by God to live out what his grace, forgiveness, and authority entail. When you stand strong for what you believe, you stand on shoulders that stretch back to the beginning—to ones that rubbed shoulders with Jesus himself.

Discussion Questions

1. What are some ways the present culture prizes diversity?
2. When is a culture's love for diversity a positive, and when is it a problem for those who believe in absolute truth?
3. How do the passages cited in this chapter imply that the early church was careful to distinguish between true and false beliefs?

7

A Likely Story

How Do We Know Jesus Rose from the Dead?

But then something else happened. Some of them began to say that God had intervened and brought him back from the dead. The story caught on, and some (or all—we don't know) of his closest followers came to think that in fact he had been raised.
—Bart Ehrman[1]

As far as I am concerned, the historian may and must say that all other explanations for why Christianity arose, and why it took the shape it did, are far less convincing as historical explanations than the one the early Christians themselves offer: that Jesus really did rise from the dead on Easter morning, leaving an empty tomb behind him.
—N. T. Wright[2]

You may not have known where all you'd be going when you started this book—deep between the lines of overblown Bible contradictions, on-site for the construction of the biblical canon, into the candlelit archives of ancient manuscripts and beyond. We hope you've found the journey to be as encouraging as it is interesting, discovering that your faith is grounded in a safe place, both relationally and intellectually.

Our truth tour can't be finished, however, until we make one final stop.

At the empty tomb.

There's a chance that some of the issues you've been scouring within these pages won't even come up in your particular slate of religion courses, won't be part of your class notes and lectures. But there's no way we can bypass the subject of Jesus' resurrection. In the war between truth and doubt, nothing outweighs the battle over a certain plot of Jerusalem-area real estate where death moved in on a Friday afternoon and came out the front door big as life on a Sunday morning.

If one changes the narrative there, then Christianity is wiped off the map. All that's left is a strange yet intriguing man of the Middle East, executed for his radical yet apparently kind-hearted beliefs.[3] Good for well-rounded reading, but hardly for building one's life around. Dead religious history.

Deal with it.

So as we reach this concluding chapter, the stakes of faith could not be higher. But be confident of this: you can step out onto the public square with much more than your copy of the New Testament and your baptism certificate. We're here to equip you with the finer points of thoughtful rebuttal and reason on a topic of key biblical importance. People may dismiss your opinions as the blind hopes of baseless tradition—which is their right to assert—but they won't just get a blank stare in return, not from *your* desk. They'll get *you*. With your answers.

And there's a lot of truth in what you'll have to say.

A Body in Motion

The starting point for all argument against doubtful views of the resurrection is the empty tomb itself. Whatever theory makes the most sense to skeptics on any given day, their chosen model must at least involve the reality of an opened grave. Because when the story began circulating in the hours following Jesus' death, suggesting that he had been miraculously raised from the dead, one quick swing out to his final resting place would have been the only, simple, falling-off-a-log requirement to stop all this fanatical discussion. One body meant no story.

Move along, everybody.

But obviously this wasn't the case. People can make whatever conjecture they please about the resurrection, from saying his body was probably stolen to wondering if it was ever actually placed there to begin with. But the tomb *was* empty. Somehow. By someone's hand. The fact that we're still talking about it today is ample proof of that. If nothing else seems to wash about the disciples' claim that Jesus came back to life after his crucifixion, the empty tomb at least remains a check in the asset column for them. It's consistent with their statement, whether you believe any of the rest of it or not.

The Bible—which obviously doesn't carry much weight with some—does include a description of Jewish officials immediately appealing to the Roman authorities upon Jesus' death to guard the tomb from any possible acts of hooliganism (Matt. 27:62–66). And when the astonishing Sunday morning news landed with a thud on the doorstep of the priests, they hastily located some funds in their rainy-day budget to bribe the Roman security detail, making sure the agreed-upon story involved tomb raiders running off with a body under cover of darkness (Matt. 28:11–15).[4] Sounds like a logical cover-up.

But on no reasonable grounds can anyone claim that Jesus' bones remained in Jesus' tomb, not by the third day after his death. The best we can tell, no one ever claimed to find Jesus' body or decayed remains. That would have ended all debate immediately. An empty tomb meant other options had to be raised. Fill-in-the-blank became the alternative.

Let's see where the doubters take us from there.

Seeing Things: The Hallucination Theory

The first of two major alternatives we'll address in this chapter involves the claim that Jesus' disciples fell under a grief-induced trance and only *imagined* they saw Jesus alive— visibly present, speaking with them, grasping them around the shoulders, smiling, laughing, settling them down, cooking their breakfast. It's a lot for them to dream up, covering nearly a month and a half of face-to-face experiences, but that's the proposition as it stands—that he was only there in their mind's eye.

These men, you'll recall, had walked away from profitable careers and family connections three years earlier to align themselves with a traveling mystic. But as time went along, their observations and expectations had become much bigger than they'd envisioned when they first set out on this spiritual journey. This man who had invited them to follow him wasn't just a convincing religious teacher. This was the Son of God. Their long-awaited Messiah. At least that's what he said, and they had grown to believe it from what they'd seen and heard and felt stirring within their hearts. Imagine what it was like being on a first-name basis with this man!

So his death, hard enough under any circumstances, was an unbearable blow to their lives and their futures. Mentally, spiritually, physically, emotionally. It's not hard to see, the skeptics say, how the disciples closest to Jesus could have become disoriented enough in mind—and desperate enough in their coping strategies—to perhaps conjure him up in a waking dream.

OK. Maybe that could happen. Rarely. Occasionally.

But could eleven people (the number of remaining apostles after the suicide of Judas) all experience the same hallucination? What about when *five hundred* people were on hand to see Jesus, all at the same time (1 Cor. 15:6)? Were the hallucinogens being passed around to every person in attendance? Was every one of his postresurrection appearances conducted at some outdoor music festival?

And what about this? When Paul was knocked to the ground while traveling the road to Damascus, en route to rounding up followers of Jesus and returning them to prison in Jerusalem, *he* certainly wasn't in a state of grief. He hated the very ground Jesus had walked on and couldn't have been happier to see him and his followers marching a steady drumbeat to the graveyard. The vivid sight and sound of the risen Christ caught Paul completely out of the blue—the last thing he was possibly expecting. Where's the rationality in saying he was lost in a fog of altered emotions?

And besides, the hallucination theory still doesn't do anything about the empty tomb, which had previously been sealed shut with a stone door and without a Jedi Master in sight. You don't just dream that into reality. Therefore, the absence of Jesus' body works against the delirium hypothesis and in favor of the disciples' account.

Think Fast: The Fabrication Theory

In addition to this head-tripping scenario, another common supposition simply calls out the followers of Christ as liars. Their Jesus was dead, and they had some explaining to do. So by quickly going into tap-dancing mode, they went about creating a hoax they prayed would buy them enough time until they could figure out their next move—and then figure out how to keep selling it going forward. Making it up as they went along.

This had better be good.

Stealing the body, of course, was obviously a big part of pulling this off. One wonders how a small band of otherwise honest men could hastily throw together the equivalent of a jewel heist, especially since they hadn't even considered the notion forty-eight hours prior, and since the scheme would require holding off a regiment of Roman soldiers who possessed far more swashbuckling skill and the heavy blades to back it up. Actually, of course, they'd need to avoid any detection by the security forces whatsoever, executing the crime with Navy Seal precision. Get in, get out, without being seen.

So the step between mapping out their plan and putting it into successful action was a doozy. But assuming you've seen enough *Mission Impossible* movies to consider this scenario within the realm of belief, let's add an extra wrinkle of historical difficulty to the mix: Jesus' death had basically shot the whole Messiah thing in the head. This meant that cooking up a resurrection story not only should never have registered on anyone's radar; it would not have been viewed by any of his followers as a plus in trying to spin public opinion. Hardly worth the effort of what amounted to a suicide mission.

Two reasons it wouldn't work: *messianic expectations* and *resurrection theology.*

The reason so many Jews dismissed Jesus as poor Messiah material all along was because he didn't fit the militaristic, world-domination model they'd always believed this person would convey. And now that he was dead, his resurrection wouldn't do anything to raise the value of his stock in their eyes. Based on what they'd seen of him the first go-around, they wouldn't expect even Jesus 2.0 to become their national deliverer. Time to start looking for somebody else. So nothing about his tragic death (*tragic* from the viewpoint of his apostles and followers) set itself up to lead naturally into the crafting of a resurrection myth. As a winning plot twist, this one just didn't hold any promise for either believability or effectiveness. The Jews would never buy it.

And neither would anyone else. The prevailing religious thought about death in *non*-Jewish culture—based on a premise that the soul was good and the physical body was bad—saw the resulting separation of soul from body as an overall positive in the long run. So in the wholly unlikely event of a person's resurrection, this reuniting of the spiritual with the physical would have been seen as not only deluded but also undesirable. The disciples just wouldn't have been inclined to think that bringing Jesus back to life (wink, wink) should be expected to play well in the wider worldview.

Jewish theology on the subject of resurrection was different, of course. And the transformation was national, collective, personal, and individual. It was designed to change everything. What's more, this coming resurrection was to coincide with a renewal of the entire world, where humankind's new existence would be able to inhabit a completely new experience. They never dreamed of someone coming back to life in the middle of flawed human history, expected to live out their rejuvenated days amid the same problems and conflicts that were here when they'd departed. Even his disciples, on those occasions when Jesus had predicted his death and resurrection, primarily seemed just to shake their heads and wonder where in the world he was getting this stuff.

Bottom line, nobody in first-century culture either expected or wanted what this alleged story was advertising. Perhaps if the disciples knew people would have found the resurrection story line attractive, albeit hard to swallow, we could reasonably keep tracking down the path of this fabrication theory. But without seeing much point in their doing it, the only good question to ask is, "Why *would* they?"

Jesus was actually not the first person in history who had gathered around him a devoted following, announcing himself the Messiah, only to be killed for daring to make such an audacious declaration. Nevertheless, as N. T. Wright observes: "In not one single case do we hear the slightest mention of the disappointed followers claiming that their hero had been raised from the dead. They knew better. Resurrection was not a private event. Jewish revolutionaries whose leader had been executed by the authorities, and who managed to escape arrest themselves, had two options: give up the revolution or find another leader. Claiming that the original leader was alive again was simply not an option. Unless, of course, he was."[5]

Yes, unless he was. Because people can run on steam for a little while. Experience tells us (if we allow ourselves to entertain this whole line of fabrication theory) that Jesus' followers could've kept up the playacting for a period of time if they were so inclined to live a desperate lie. But eventually the weight of maintaining their story, rolling it consistently forward, and keeping everybody on board—it finally submarines the charade. A lie, after all, is a terrible thing to live.

It's an even harder thing to die for.

And yet that's exactly what happened—not just in a few isolated cases but across the spectrum, in ever increasing waves, continuing on across the years and generations. Those who choose today to reject the resurrection of Jesus, who consider it a contrived attempt by his disciples at creating a Christ legend, must be able to explain "how a small band of defeated followers of Jesus were transformed almost overnight into bold witnesses, risking death by proclaiming his bodily resurrection before many of the same people who fifty days earlier had participated in his crucifixion."[6]

They *can't* explain it. Who could?

"While many have died for their convictions," writes apologist and author Gary Habermas, "Jesus' disciples were in the right place to know the truth or falsity of the event for which they were willing to die."[7] They were self-destructive to the max, every last one of them, if they were prepared to follow their pack of lies all the way to the torture rack. Reason would argue they would only carry it so far . . . and no farther. Yet they carried it for the rest of their lives, never free from jail time and persecution.

Oh, and here's another thing. Consider this a final clincher, if none of the others seem to be getting you anywhere. The usual pattern when concocting a piece of hasty fiction (assuming you don't have a working knowledge of this practice!) is to overthink the scene. In trying to foolproof it, to build a watertight case, you add layers of detail you would expect your audience (your parents, your teacher, your boyfriend/girlfriend) to believe and accept. Since you're not simply reporting on what actually happened, the canvas of possibilities is wide. And deceptive human nature compels us to fill it up.

What kind of lunacy, then, would direct the fast-thinking followers of Jesus to build out his resurrection fraud by leaving themselves out of the starring roles? For example, if a first-century Jew were intent on making up a good story, it certainly wouldn't feature women as prominent characters. Women weren't even permitted to testify in a court of law at this period in history, except in specific cases like sexual abuse.[8] They would hardly have made the most believable eyewitnesses and first responders to the risen Christ, not in the first draft of the script, the second draft, or *any* draft that was hurriedly agreed upon in the apostles' underground writing sessions.

To make matters even *more* misaligned, the Eleven are shown in one account as calling these ladies crazy for implying such a thing. "These words seemed like nonsense to them," the Bible says, "and they did not believe the women" (Luke 24:11). This is hardly the promising pose you'd want them to strike if your main objective was to convince everyone else these events actually happened.

So you've got an unlikely story, an unimpressed audience, risks of an untimely death, and a totally uncommon cast of characters. The claim is the disciples fabricated a culturally unpopular idea (resurrection), using people who do not count as witnesses for it (women), presented to a host of unbelieving followers (doubting disciples) as the way to persuade a doubting audience. Not one of these elements passes the smell test for the fabrication theory. And they do nothing to make a dent in the much more reasonable account—even if no more believable to a doubting mind—that Jesus, by the most astounding earthly miracle of all, came up out of a grave in a resurrected body.

Supernaturally Skeptical

There are other arguments as well. Some believe Jesus wasn't really dead but was only in an unconscious swoon. Others say his postresurrection persona was an imposter, a stand-in or lookalike, or perhaps that he came back in some kind of spiritual form that didn't actually equate to coming back physically from the dead. But at the heart of these claims and all the rest is a baseline skepticism against all things supernatural. If nothing but grief trauma, mental delusions, and conspiratorial theatrics are allowed to populate the universe of acceptable theories, then a person is deliberately choosing to limit how big their choices are able to be.

But that's not the same as saying they're limiting themselves to what's *reasonable* because none of these alternative propositions are reasonable. They each fail to accommodate an empty tomb. Or if they do, they fail on any number of other fronts, as we've just seen. Like it or not, the most *reasonable* story is the one declared as fact in our Bibles. And the fact that it's *supernatural* shouldn't disqualify it from consideration, not unless you're simply biased from accepting a position that shatters the far reaches of the five senses.

The only remaining question to ask: "Is the biblical account of Christ's resurrection reasonable?"

Well, yes . . . it is.

And you can walk this conclusion into any conversation in the country, confident you've thought your way all around the issues, confident you're not just believing by blind faith, confident your belief in Christ has truth and reason on its side. That's not to say you'll pull everybody else over to your way of thinking. But neither are you reduced to "covering your ears and humming loudly" as Ehrman refers to his students so as not to be throttled by the assault of doubt. We close this chapter with the astute observation by Tim Keller:

> Each year at Easter I get to preach on the
> Resurrection. In my sermon I always say to my
> skeptical, secular friends, that even if they can't
> believe in the resurrection, they should want
> it to be true. Most of them care deeply about
> justice for the poor, alleviating hunger and

disease, and caring for the environment. Yet, many of them believe that the material world was caused by accident and that the world and everything in it will eventually simply burn up in the death of the sun. They find it discouraging that so few people care about justice without realizing that their own worldview undermines any motivation to make the world a better place. Why sacrifice for the needs of others if in the end nothing we do will make any differences? If the resurrection of Jesus happened, however, that means there's infinite hope and reason to pour ourselves out for the needs of the world.[9]

Well said. And ready to be well lived.

Discussion Questions

1. What are some of the alternative explanations for the empty tomb and claims made by eyewitnesses that Jesus rose from the dead? What are some of the problems with these alternative explanations?
2. What is significant about women being the first eyewitnesses to the resurrection?
3. Why, according to Tim Keller, should even skeptics want the resurrection to be true?

A Good Read on Reasoned Faith

B art Ehrman tells the following story of how he often begins his university classes:

> The first day of class, with over three hundred students present, I ask: "How many of you would agree with the proposition that the Bible is the inspired Word of God?" *Whoosh!* Virtually everyone in the auditorium raises their hand. I then ask, "How many of you have one or more of the Harry Potter books?" *Whoosh!* The whole auditorium. Then I ask, "And how many of you have read the entire Bible?" Scattered hands, a few students here and there. I always laugh and say, "Okay, look. I'm not saying that I think God wrote the Bible. You're telling me that *you* think God wrote the Bible. I can see why you might want to read a book by J. K. Rowling. But if God wrote a book . . . wouldn't you want to see what he has to say?"[1]

We couldn't have made the point better ourselves. The challenge for everyone who thinks the Bible is (or even is possibly) inspired by God is to actually read it. Before reading any books that seek to call it into question—before even engrossing yourself in books like this one, which argues hard for a defense of Scripture—*read the Bible!*

- See for yourself how it addresses the problem of sin and its effect on the world around us. And judge for yourself whether it corresponds with the world around you.
- See for yourself the compassion of Jesus and the great authority of his words.
- See for yourself the remarkable unity among the diverse human authors.
- See for yourself the majesty and beauty of the God who did not leave the world to shrivel up and die but has initiated a plan to redeem his creation and make things right once again.

From the beginning of this book, we have noted the difference between blind faith and reasoned faith. We have constantly reminded you that Christianity never asks anyone to believe something that's not true just for the sake of believing. But as you launch out from this one experience to the next adventure on your journey, we encourage you to take the comfort and confidence of a reasoned faith beyond the challenge of the skeptic and into the rhythm of your everyday life.

One danger—very subtle—of sinking so deeply into the mission of defending your faith is to reduce belief to intellectual acceptance. The sky is blue, the grass is green, and Jesus rose from the dead, stated as if they're each of equal importance and consequence. No, your faith in Christ is not only well placed because it makes reasonable sense, against all other worldviews and patterns of thought, but because this Jesus can change *you* and *us* and inspire us to lives that brim with our created purpose.

Reasoned faith is all-purpose faith. It not only operates from a school desk but from every place you sit and stand and live and interact. Use this fresh assurance in God and his Word to let it soak all the way through you—through your heart as well as your head. Submit to him with your whole being, allowing him steadily to mature you and prepare you for each new sunrise and opportunity of life, including the problems and the hard places.

And stay in the Scripture, not merely to prove it true but to show it alive and enlightening, transforming you into someone who thinks and acts and speaks and responds with Christlike character because of the Holy Spirit that works inside you.

The God whose eternal truth and nature stand behind the Bible is not only your champion as you claim that truth matters but also for your heart and soul as a devoted believer. Be his disciple as well as his defender, and you will love the places your reasoned faith in him can take you.

You will know the truth, and the truth will set you free.
JOHN 8:32

Discussion Questions

1. How can you make sure you stay in the Scriptures so that when questions come you know what the Bible teaches on a given subject?

2. Are you involved in a healthy church? How can you contribute?

3. What is the best way to deal with skeptics who question the accuracy of the Bible? Have you had any opportunities lately to address with others the kinds of issues covered in this book?

Digging Deeper

Truth Matters is an introduction to the topic of how skeptics approach Scripture. It discusses key ideas and principles to help readers understand and respond to these objections. But many details are not present here.

So for those who wish to dig deeper, we have written a more detailed version called *Truth in a Culture of Doubt* (releasing in Fall 2014), which includes fuller documentation and support. This latter book will give you a larger look at the rationale for the arguments offered here. You may also find it helpful to share this more detailed version with someone you know who wants to go even deeper on this subject.

Our hope is that these resources will help you answer your own questions and the questions of others.

Notes

Preface

1. Bart D. Ehrman, *Jesus, Interrupted: Revealing the Hidden Contradictions in the Bible (And Why We Don't Know about Them)* (San Francisco: HarperOne, 2009), 14.

Chapter 1

1. Bart D. Ehrman, *Did Jesus Exist? The Historical Argument for Jesus of Nazareth* (San Francisco: HarperOne, 2012), 142.

2. Bart D. Ehrman, *Misquoting Jesus: The Story Behind Who Changed the Bible and Why* (San Francisco: Harper, 2005); *God's Problem: How the Bible Fails to Answer Our Most Important Question—Why We Suffer* (New York: HarperCollins, 2008); *Jesus, Interrupted: Revealing the Hidden Contradictions in the Bible (And Why We Don't Know About Them)* (San Francisco: HarperOne, 2009); *Forged: Writing in the Name of God—Why the Bible's Authors Are Not Who We Think They Are* (San Francisco, HarperOne, 2011).

3. Ehrman, *God's Problem*, 127.

4. Ehrman, *Misquoting Jesus*, 10.

5. D. A. Carson, *The Intolerance of Tolerance* (Grand Rapids: Eerdmans, 2012), 97 (emphasis added).

6. Ehrman, *God's Problem*, 4.

7. Ehrman, *Jesus, Interrupted*, 17.

8. Michael J. Kruger, "Review of Bart D. Ehrman, *Jesus, Interrupted*, *Westminster Theological Journal* 71, no. 2 (2009): 502–9. ATS (the Association of Theological Schools) is the agency that accredits many seminaries in the United States.

9. Ehrman, *Did Jesus Exist?*, 143–44.

Chapter 2

1. Bart D. Ehrman, *God's Problem: How the Bible Fails to Answer Our Most Important Question—Why We Suffer* (New York: HarperCollins, 2008), 16.

2. Timothy Keller, *The Reason for God: Belief in an Age of Skepticism* (New York: Penguin, 2008), 23–24.

3. Ehrman, *God's Problem*, 66.

4. Ibid., 128.

5. Keller, *The Reason for God*, 24.

6. Ehrman, *God's Problem*, 13.

7. Ibid., 13.

8. Alvin Plantinga, "A Christian Life Partly Lived," in *Philosophers Who Believe: The Spiritual Journeys of 11 Leading Thinkers*, ed. Kelly James Clark (Downers Grove: InterVarsity, 1997), 72.

9. Alister E. McGrath, *Mere Apologetics: How to Help Seekers and Skeptics Find Faith* (Grand Rapids: Baker, 2012), 166–67.

10. Keller, *The Reason for God*, 74–75.

11. McGrath, *Mere Apologetics*, 166.

Chapter 3

1. Bart D. Ehrman, *Lost Christianities: The Battles for Scripture and the Faiths We Never Knew* (Oxford: Oxford University Press, 2003), 248.

2. Michael Kruger, review of Bart D. Ehrman, *Jesus, Interrupted*, *Westminster Journal* 71, no. 2 (2009): 502–9.

3. Daniel Radosh, "The Good Book Business," http://www.new yorker.com/archive/2006/12/18/061218fa_fact1, accessed May 14, 2013.

4. Irenaeus, *Against Heresies*, 3.1.1 and 3.11.8.

5. See Bruce M. Metzger, *The Canon of the New Testament* (Oxford: Clarendon, 1987), 305–7.

6. Ibid.

7. Ibid., 172.

8. Ibid., 173.

9. *Catechesis*, 6.31.

10. *Hom. in Luc*, 1.

11. Andreas J. Köstenberger and Michael J. Kruger, *Heresy of Orthodoxy: How Contemporary Culture's Fascination with Diversity Has Reshaped Our Understanding of Early Christianity* (Wheaton, IL: Crossway, 2010), 166. See also Darrell Bock and Daniel Wallace, *Dethroning Jesus: Exposing Popular Culture's Quest to Unseat the Biblical Christ* (Nashville: Thomas Nelson, 2007), 113–22.

12. Richard Bauckham, *Jesus and the Eyewitnesses: The Gospels as Eyewitness Testimony* (Grand Rapids: Eerdmans, 2006).

13. Incidentally, you'll look in vain for references to Bauckham's work in Ehrman's writings on the subject.

14. Ehrman, *Forged: Writing in the Name of God—Why the Bible's Authors Are Not Who We Think They Are* (San Francisco, HarperOne, 2011), 75.

15. See Craig Evans, "Jewish Scripture and the Literacy of Jesus," accessed 10 October 2013 at http://www.craigaevans.com/evans.pdf, and Alan Millard, *Reading and Writing in the Time of Jesus*, The Biblical Seminar 69 (Sheffield Academic Press, 2000).

16. Ben Witherington III, "Bart Interrupted," http://benwitherington.blogspot.com/2009/04.

17. Michael Kruger, "The Authenticity of 2 Peter," *Journal of the Evangelical Theological Society* 42 (1999): 670.

18. Michael Licona, "Review of *Forged: Writing in the Name of God—Why the Bible's Authors Are Not Who We Think They Are*," 2–3. Posted online at http://www.risenjesus.com/articles/52-review-of-forged, accessed June 21, 2012.

Chapter 4

1. Bart Ehrman, *Jesus, Interrupted: Revealing the Hidden Contradictions in the Bible (And Why We Don't Know About Them* (San Francisco: HarperOne, 2009), 16.

2. Ben Witherington III, "Bart Interrupted," http://benwitherington .blogspot.com/2009/04/bart-interrupted-part-four.html, accessed March 25, 2010.

3. See, e.g., *Gospel of Nicodemus 2*, which repeats the charge of Jesus' birth being the result of fornication; and Origen, *Against Celsus* 1.28, according to which Jesus' birth was the result of Mary's sexual union with Panthera, a Roman soldier.

4. Andreas J. Köstenberger, "John's Transposition Theology: Retelling the Story of Jesus in a Different Key," in *Earliest Christian History*, ed. Michael F. Bird and Jason Maston, Wissenschaftliche Untersuchungen zum Neuen Testament 2/320 (Tübingen: Mohr Siebeck, 2012), 191–226.

5. In fact, there is one "sign" of Jesus in the other Gospels, the "sign of Jonah" (Matt. 12:38–45). Could it be that that's where John got the idea?

6. See Köstenberger, "John's Transposition Theology."

7. Ehrman, *Jesus, Interrupted*, 89–90.

8. Ibid., 90.

9. D. A. Carson, *Jesus' Sermon on the Mount and His Confrontation with the World: An Exposition of Matthew 5–10* (Grand Rapids: Baker, 2004), 128. For an example of a responsible, less dichotomous treatment on the relationship between Paul and Jesus, see David Wenham, *Paul: Founder of Christianity or Follower of Jesus?* (Grand Rapids: Eerdmans, 1996).

10. See the original Greek titles of the four Gospels: "The Gospel according to Matthew," "The Gospel according to Mark," "The Gospel according to Luke," and "The Gospel according to John."

11. Bart Ehrman, *Misquoting Jesus: The Story Behind Who Changed the Bible and Why* (San Francisco: Harper, 2005), 9.

12. Ibid., 11.

13. Michael J. Kruger, "Review of Bart D. Ehrman, *Jesus, Interrupted*, *Westminster Theological Journal* 71, no. 2 (2009): 502–9.

14. Richard Bauckham, *God Crucified: Monotheism and Christology in the New Testament* (Grand Rapids: Wm. B. Eerdmans, 1999), 24; cf. Andreas J. Köstenberger, *A Theology of John's Gospel and Letters: The Word, the Christ, the Son of God* (Biblical Theology of the New Testament; Grand Rapids: Zondervan, 2009), 356–60.

15. N. T. Wright, *Jesus and the Victory of God* (Minneapolis: Fortress, 1997). For a helpful summary of his argument concerning the deity of Jesus in *Jesus and the Victory of God*, see N. T. Wright, appendix to Antony Flew, *There Is a God* (New York: Harper Collins, 2007), 188–95; and Marcus Borg and N. T. Wright, *The Meaning of Jesus: Two Visions* (New York: Harper, 1999), 157–68.

16. Wright, *Jesus and the Victory of God*, 623.

17. Wright, "Appendix B," in Flew, *Jesus: Two Visions*, 190–91.

18. Ibid., 192.

19. Darrell L. Bock, *Blasphemy and Exaltation in Judaism and the Jewish Examination of Jesus* (Wissenschaftliche Untersuchungen zum Neuen Testament 2; Tübingen: Mohr Siebeck, 2009).

20. D. A. Carson, *The Gospel according to John*, Pillar New Testament Commentary (Grand Rapids: Eerdmans, 1991), 57.

21. Andreas Köstenberger, "Diversity and Unity in the New Testament," in *Biblical Theology: Retrospect & Prospect*, ed. Scott J. Hafemann (Downers Grove: InterVarsity, 2002), 154–58.

22. G. B. Caird, *New Testament Theology*, ed. L. D. Hurst (Oxford: Clarendon, 1994), 24.

Chapter 5

1. Bart D. Ehrman, in *The Reliability of the New Testament: Bart D. Ehrman & Daniel B. Wallace in Dialogue*, ed. Robert B. Stewart (Minneapolis: Fortress, 2011), 14.

2. Mark D. Roberts, *Can We Trust the Gospels? Investigating the Reliability of Matthew, Mark, Luke, and John* (Wheaton: Crossway, 2007), 37.

3. For further examples, see "Table 1.1: Extant Copies of Ancient Works," Andreas J. Köstenberger, L. Scott Kellum, and Charles L.

Quarles, *Cradle, the Cross, and the Crown: An Introduction to the New Testament* (Nashville: B&H Academic, 2009), 34.

4. Bruce M. Metzger and Bart D. Ehrman, *The Text of the New Testament: Its Transmission, Corruption, and Restoration*, 4th ed. (New York: Oxford University Press, 2005), 86.

5. "Can We Trust the Text of the New Testament? A Debate between Daniel B. Wallace and Bart D. Ehrman," October 1, 2011; DVD; Dallas: Center for the Study of New Testament Manuscripts, 2011.

6. Andreas J. Köstenberger and Michael J. Kruger, *Heresy of Orthodoxy: How Contemporary Culture's Fascination with Diversity Has Reshaped Our Understanding of Early Christianity* (Wheaton, IL: Crossway, 2010), 210–11.

7. There is a single manuscript of *Jewish War* from the third century, but it is practically illegible and only a small fragment.

8. The following list gives some of our earliest New Testament manuscripts ($\mathcal{P}$ is the symbol for "papyrus").

- $\mathcal{P}$52: manuscript containing John 18:31–33, 37–38 from around AD 125
- $\mathcal{P}$90: manuscript containing John 18:36–19:7 from the second century
- $\mathcal{P}$104: manuscript containing Matthew 21:34–37, 43, 45(?) from the second century
- $\mathcal{P}$66: manuscript of John from the late second century
- $\mathcal{P}$98: manuscript containing Revelation 1 from the second century
- $\mathcal{P}$4, $\mathcal{P}$64=$\mathcal{P}$67: manuscripts containing Luke 1–6 and Matthew 3; 5; 26 from the late second century
- $\mathcal{P}$46: manuscript of most Pauline epistles from approximately AD 200 (Rom. 5–6; 8–16; 1–2 Corinthians; Galatians; Ephesians; Philippians; Colossians; 1 Thessalonians; and Hebrews [grouped with the Pauline corpus])
- $\mathcal{P}$103: manuscript containing Matthew 13–14 from approximately AD 200

- $\mathcal{P}$75: manuscript containing Luke 3–18; 22–24; and John 1–15 from approximately AD 200–225

9. Ehrman repeatedly emphasized this point in the debate "Can We Trust the Text of the New Testament? A Debate between Daniel B. Wallace & Bart D. Ehrman."

10. Adapted from Köstenberger and Kruger, *Heresy of Orthodoxy*, 211.

11. For a succinct introduction to textual criticism, see Bruce M. Metzger, *A Textual Commentary on the Greek New Testament*, 2d ed. (New York: UBS, 1994), 1–16.

12. Bart D. Ehrman, *Misquoting Jesus: The Story Behind Who Changed the Bible and Why* (San Francisco: Harper, 2005), 208.

13. Daniel Wallace, "The Gospel According to Bart: A Review Article of *Misquoting Jesus* by Bart Ehrman," *Journal of the Evangelical Theological Society* 49 (2006): 339.

14. Or perhaps better, "One and Only, [himself] God" (or "God in his own right"). The point is not that Jesus was the *only* God (as if God the Father were not God) but that Jesus, the One and Only Son of God, was divine as well. See Andreas J. Köstenberger, *John*, Baker Exegetical Commentary on the New Testament (Grand Rapids: Baker Academic, 2004), 49–50; idem, *A Theology of John's Gospel and Letters: The Word, the Christ, the Son of God* (Biblical Theology of the New Testament; Grand Rapids: Zondervan, 2009), 381–82.

15. Roberts, *Can We Trust the Gospels?*, 33–34.

16. Ehrman, *Misquoting Jesus*, 207.

17. For more on handwriting and ancient scribes, see Köstenberger and Kruger, *Heresy of Orthodoxy*, 186–90.

18. Harry Y. Gamble, *Books and Readers in the Early Church* (New Haven, CT: Yale University Press, 1995), 91.

19. T. C. Skeat, "Early Christian Book-Production," in *The Cambridge History of the Bible*, vol. 2 (Cambridge: Cambridge University Press, 1969), 73.

20. Köstenberger and Kruger, *Heresy of Orthodoxy*, 195.

21. Ehrman, *Misquoting Jesus*, 7.

22. Ibid., 211.

23. Peter Williams, "Review of Bart Ehrman, *Misquoting Jesus*," http://evangelicaltextualcriticism.blogspot.com/2005/12/review-of-bart -ehrman-misquoting-jesus_31.html.

Chapter 6

1. Bart D. Ehrman, *Jesus, Interrupted: Revealing the Hidden Contradictions in the Bible (And Why We Don't Know about Them)* (San Francisco: HarperOne, 2009), 215.

2. D. A. Carson, back cover endorsement of Andreas J. Köstenberger and Michael J. Kruger, *Heresy of Orthodoxy: How Contemporary Culture's Fascination with Diversity Has Reshaped Our Understanding of Early Christianity* (Wheaton, IL: Crossway, 2010).

3. This view is not only one among a plethora of conspiracy theories so prevalent in American culture; it is also exceedingly cynical: Christianity is based on nothing more than beliefs that proved expedient for the powerful—and the actual truth (i.e., religious diversity!) was brutally suppressed by those who knew better. See on this David R. Liefeld, "God's Word or Male Words? Postmodern Conspiracy Culture and Feminist Myths of Christian Origins," *Journal of the Evangelical Theological Society* 48, no. 3 (2005): 449–73. See also Craig A. Blaising, "Faithfulness: A Prescription for Theology," in *Quo Vadis, Evangelicalism? Perspectives on the Past, Direction for the Future: Nine Presidential Addresses from the First Fifty Years of the Journal of the Evangelical Theological Society* (Wheaton: Crossway, 2007), 201–16.

4. Bart D. Ehrman, *Lost Christianities: The Battles for Scripture and the Faiths We Never Knew* (Oxford: Oxford University Press, 2003), 173.

5. For a fuller refutation of the Bauer thesis, see Köstenberger and Kruger, *Heresy of Orthodoxy*, chapters 1 and 2.

6. Darrell L. Bock, *The Missing Gospels: Unearthing the Truth behind Alternative Christianities* (Nashville: Thomas Nelson, 2007), 50.

7. The only first-century evidence for controversy reveals some Jewish groups who embraced Jesus but questioned his deity (the Ebionites).

8. The classic treatment on Gnosticism is Edwin Yamauchi, *Pre-Christian Gnosticism: A Survey of the Proposed Evidences* (Grand Rapids: Eerdmans, 1973). See further below.

9. See Köstenberger and Kruger, *Heresy of Orthodoxy*, chapter 3, esp. 89–98.

10. For a survey of the major sects of the second century, see Antti Marjanen and Petri Luomanen, eds., *A Companion to Second-Century Christian "Heretics,"* Supplements to Vigiliae Christianae 76 (Leiden: Brill, 2005).

11. Paul embarked on at least three missionary journeys, commonly dated to the years 47–48, 49–51, and 51–54. See, e.g., Andreas J. Köstenberger, L. Scott Kellum, and Charles L. Quarles, *Cradle, the Cross, and the Crown: An Introduction to the New Testament* (Nashville: B&H Academic, 2009), 391–94.

12. Michael B. Thompson, "The Holy Internet: Communication between Churches in the First Christian Generation," in Richard Bauckham, ed., *The Gospels for All Christians: Rethinking the Gospel Audiences* (Grand Rapids: Eerdmans, 1998), 49–70.

13. See the concluding chapter in Bock's *The Missing Gospels*, where a survey of these writings shows that almost all of them mention in one way or another what this core theology was.

14. Köstenberger and Kruger, *Heresy of Orthodoxy*, 66.

15. G. B. Caird, *New Testament Theology*, ed. L. D. Hurst (Oxford: Clarendon, 1994), 24.

16. If you want more detail, we have written a more comprehensive, scholarly book that we note later in the appendix "Digging Deeper."

Chapter 7

1. Bart D. Ehrman, *Did Jesus Exist? The Historical Argument for Jesus of Nazareth* (San Francisco: HarperOne, 2012), 164.

2. N. T. Wright, "Jesus' Resurrection and Christian Origins," online at http://ntwrightpage.com/Wright_Jesus_Resurrection.htm, accessed June 30, 2012.

3. Excellent reading on this subject includes the classic by Josh and Sean McDowell, *More Than a Carpenter* (Carol Stream, IL: Tyndale Momentum, 2009). More broadly, see C. S. Lewis, *Mere Christianity* (London: Geoffrey Bles, 1952); and Timothy Keller, *The Reason for God: Belief in an Age of Skepticism* (New York: Penguin, 2008).

4. Even Mary Magdalene, before recognizing the resurrected Jesus for who he was, told him, "Sir, if you've removed Him [i.e., Jesus' body], tell me where you've put Him, and I will take Him away" (John 20:15; see also her earlier similar comments to the angels, John 20:13).

5. N. T. Wright, *Who Was Jesus?* (Grand Rapids: Eerdmans, 1993), 63.

6. Craig L. Blomberg, "Jesus of Nazareth: How Historians Can Know Him and Why It Matters," online at http://thegospelcoalition .org/cci/article/jesus_of_nazareth_how_historians_can_know_him _and_why_it_matters, accessed June 30, 2012. Note how in the Gospel accounts Jesus' disciples are scared to death following the crucifixion, hiding behind locked doors (John 20:19), even a week later (John 20:26).

7. Gary R. Habermas, "The Resurrection Appearances of Jesus," in Michael Licona and William A. Dembski, eds., *Evidence for God: 50 Arguments for Faith from the Bible, History, Philosophy, and Science* (Grand Rapids: Baker Books, 2010), 174–75.

8. Richard Bauckham, *Gospel Women: Studies of the Named Women in the Gospels* (Grand Rapids: Eerdmans/Edinburgh: T&T Clark, 2002), 268–77; cf. N. T. Wright, *Resurrection of the Son of God* (Christian Origins and the Question of God, vol. 3) (Minneapolis: Fortress, 2003), 607. See also ancient Jewish texts such as *m. Shebuot* 4.1; *Rosh Hashanah* 1.8; *b. Baba Qamma* 88a that show how consistent this idea was across the centuries of Jewish tradition, even after the time of Jesus.

9. Timothy Keller, *The Reason for God: Belief in an Age of Skepticism* (New York: Penguin, 2008), 220.

Epilogue

1. Bart D. Ehrman, *Jesus, Interrupted: Revealing the Hidden Contradictions in the Bible (And Why We Don't Know About Them)* (San Francisco: HarperOne, 2009), 225–26.